THE EPIDEMIOLOGY OF
DEPRESSION

THE EPIDEMIOLOGY OF
DEPRESSION

CHARLOTTE SILVERMAN, M.D., DR. P.H.

THE JOHNS HOPKINS PRESS
BALTIMORE

Copyright © 1968 by The Johns Hopkins Press
Baltimore, Maryland 21218

All rights reserved

Manufactured in the United States of America
Library of Congress Catalog Card Number 68-31639

This publication is the outcome of an extensive review and analysis of research in the field of mental health epidemiology. The original impetus for this study was a National Institute of Mental Health Research Utilization Conference on the Epidemiology of Mental Disorders in June, 1965. The author, first as Assistant Chief, Social Psychiatry Section, and later as Chief, Epidemiologic Studies Branch, National Institute of Mental Health, was responsible for developing a research and demonstration program on the epidemiology of mental disorders. The present publication, prepared subsequently, is based on work carried out as an integral part of those assignments.

TO MY MOTHER

FOREWORD

The present interest in and support of community mental health measures invites and encourages the participation of workers trained in epidemiology and other public health disciplines. There is need for conceptual bridges to achieve meaningful communication with psychiatric clinicians. The bringing together of bodies of knowledge and methods of work which are apparently unrelated may bring fresh insights and facilitate useful collaboration.

Dr. Silverman has done a splendid job in this scholarly work on depression. She has done much more than compile the literature. Semantic puzzles such as "depressive reaction" and "reactive depression" have not dismayed her. She has achieved much.

She has brought clarity of thought to a complex area. Her book is both comprehensive and comprehensible.

There may be a depressive phase in every type of mental illness. Indeed, life itself has its inevitable touches of melancholy. Societies differ in respect to definitions of success, ambition, pride, shame, and guilt. Temperaments differ in respect to moody propensities. Some are gripped by conventional compulsions with a steely grasp, others lightly disregard them. The uncommitted cannot be discouraged, because they have not known courage.

Without knowledge of life situation, background, attitudes, and expectations, it is difficult to judge and evaluate melancholy demeanor and behavior.

The overworked psychiatrist may not be greatly troubled by the complexities of understanding this whole gamut; his attention is demanded for the most frankly morbid. But the student of populations has a broader scope, in which conceptualization and enumeration are exceedingly difficult problems.

Dr. Silverman's book should be a useful guide.

JOHN C. WHITEHORN
Henry Phipps Professor Emeritus of Psychiatry
The Johns Hopkins University School of Medicine

PREFACE

Epidemiology has performed a vital role in contributing to an understanding of the communicable diseases and to their subsequent prevention and control. As the chronic diseases, including mental illness, assume an increasing position of importance as the major public health problem of our day, we would expect to see the epidemiologic study of these diseases play a primary role in the elucidation of etiologic factors, at least to the point that would allow for the development of a certain degree of prevention. To be sure, the past several decades have witnessed the gradual increase in the application of the epidemiologic approach to these diseases; as a result, epidemiologic studies have indicated the etiologic relationship between cigarette smoking and lung cancer, demonstrated the role of excess oxygen exposure in causing retrolental fibroplasia, and revealed the relationship of certain risk factors to the development of coronary heart disease. However, progress in many areas has been slow, with few accomplishments; this is particularly true in mental illness.

The potential value of epidemiologic observations in mental illness was proposed in the 1930's by Elkind, Freeman, and Emerson. An important stimulus was provided by the now classic study by Faris and Dunham; in 1939 they reported on "Mental Disorders in Urban Areas: An Ecological Study of Schizophrenia and Other Psychoses." Since then there have been numerous population surveys of various types of mental illness.

In this volume, Dr. Silverman has presented a systematic, critical, and comprehensive review on the epidemiology of one of the major forms of mental illness of our times, and has thoroughly assessed the available data on trends, prevalence, and incidence of depression. She has pointedly indicated the need for considering suicide, an area where there is a great deal of current interest from a programmatic viewpoint, as the mortality component of the disease spectrum of depression. The few studies concerned with the differential characteristics of depressed persons are also examined. Finally, Dr. Silverman offers several possible directions for further epidemiologic research which could give valuable aid in the effort to overcome existing deficiencies in our knowledge.

The mere fact that it was possible to prepare this volume attests to the interest that does exist in the epidemiology of mental disease. Nonetheless, it must be admitted that this interest has been quite sporadic and limited. There has been an unwarranted hesitancy on the part of workers in this area to think beyond the population survey technique and utilize other available methodologic approaches in focusing on a specific type of mental disorder.

PREFACE

Dr. Silverman's initiative in meeting this challenge has provided an excellent review incorporating the necessary integrated background knowledge which can be used as the base for a broad epidemiologic research program. It is hoped that it will stimulate the interest of epidemiologists, behavioral scientists, and psychiatrists in this important research area, and, perhaps, from this increased awareness of the potential value of epidemiological knowledge, the much needed integrated research program will develop. One can also hope that similar stimulating reviews will be prepared, to give additional insight into other mental diseases.

ABRAHAM M. LILIENFELD
Professor of Chronic Diseases
The Johns Hopkins University School
of Hygiene and Public Health

ACKNOWLEDGMENTS

The author wishes to express her deep gratitude to the many individuals who directly or indirectly contributed to this volume. She is particularly indebted to certain colleagues for specific assistance as indicated below.

To the following members of the staff of the National Institute of Mental Health: Dr. Morton Kramer and his associates for their generous provision of biometric data and source materials; Mrs. Katharine B. Wolpe for her unstinting assistance in obtaining and making available reference articles and books from the NIMH library, the library of the National Institutes of Health, the National Library of Medicine and other sources; Mr. Walter Clark for his preparation of graphs which strikingly illustrate the successful blending of accuracy and artistry; and most especially Mrs. Catharine G. Marceron for her invaluable and dedicated help in typing and editing the manuscript and in preparing the bibliography, without whom this book would never have evolved to its present form. Above all, to Dr. Caroline Chandler, friend and colleague, for her critical counsel and unerring judgments throughout the entire gestation period.

To Dr. Paul V. Lemkau and Dr. Abraham M. Lilienfeld of the faculty of The Johns Hopkins University School of Hygiene and Public Health: to the former, for his careful and helpful review of the initial draft; to the latter, for his critical review of a later draft and for his preparation of the important Preface to this book. To Dr. John C. Whitehorn, The Johns Hopkins University School of Medicine, for writing the Foreword, which speaks eloquently for itself.

To the participants in the small work conference on the epidemiology of mental disorders held in Bethesda in June, 1965, which was the beginning of this undertaking: Dr. John C. Cassel, Dr. John A. Clausen, Dr. Jonathan O. Cole, Dr. Seymour S. Kety, Dr. Morton Kramer, Dr. Abraham M. Lilienfeld, and Dr. John C. Whitehorn.

To the American Psychiatric Association for the opportunity to present a small part of the material on morbidity and mortality at the annual meeting in May, 1967, and to the *American Journal of Psychiatry* for publishing this in January, 1968 (Silverman, C.: The Epidemiology of Depression—A Review. *Amer. J. Psychiat.* 124: 883-91, 1968.).

Specific credits have been given at points of citation for tables, quotations, and data taken from the literature.

INTRODUCTION

In planning a review of the literature germane to the epidemiology of depression, it became apparent that it was no more possible to exclude the many determinants of epidemiologic findings than it was to consider depression as a discrete psychiatric entity. The result has been a rather large undertaking that has included concepts of mental disorders and depressive states; diagnostic criteria and reliability; morbidity, in terms of time trends and active prevalence and incidence; mortality (as suicide); and various personal and environmental characteristics of persons with depression. Even so, there may be unintentional omissions. In addition to analyses of reported studies and observations, recalculations have been made of most of the prevalence data and a small amount of new material presented.

Epidemiology, the study of the distribution of a disease or condition in a population and of the factors that influence this distribution (197), is both a method and a body of knowledge, an essential element in public health and medicine. The search in epidemiology is for combinations of characteristics and circumstances that distinguish the affected from the unaffected person in the population. The essence of the epidemiologic method is that the same information must be obtained about all the members of a population or its defined sample. The strategy is to test causal inferences that are derived from statistical associations between the condition being studied and individual or group attributes. The goal is to gain knowledge and understanding for prevention and control.

The depressive states, like other types of mental disturbances, are difficult to define and classify because of lack of knowledge of distinguishing and causative factors. For this reason, the term depression, instead of the name of a specific depressive condition, has been used so that the limits of this everyday and technical term could be explored without restriction. Depressive illness is regarded as second only to schizophrenia in significance as a psychiatric problem and it is of paramount concern with regard to suicide; the depressive mood is of importance in most fields of health and behavior. Relatively little attention has been given to depression in past years, but now there is heightened interest in this group of disorders, as evidenced by ongoing biochemical, psychopharmacologic, and clinical research.

C. S.

CONTENTS

Foreword vii
Preface ix
Acknowledgments xiii
Introduction xv
  I Basic Considerations 1
  II Morbidity 27
  III Mortality: Suicide 55
  IV Some Characteristics of Persons with Depression . 73
  V Perspectives for Future Research 131
Appendices 137
Selected Bibliography 153
Index 179

TEXT TABLES AND FIGURES

Table	1. Affective Disorders among Leading Diagnoses	32
Table	2. Cases and Rates of Hospitalization for Psychoses	34
Table	3. Point Prevalence of Depressive Disorders	42
Table	4. Period Prevalence of Depressive Disorders	44
Table	5. First Admissions for Depressive Disorders	51
Table	6. Depressive Disorders among Suicides	64
Table	7. Suicides in Mental Disease Patients	68
Figure	1. Affective Disorders among Leading Diagnoses	31
Figure	2. Depressive Disorders among Suicides	63
Figure	3. Suicides in Mental Disease Patients	67

APPENDIX TABLES AND FIGURES

Table	1. Depressive Disorders, 1952 Classification	137
Table	2. Depressive Disorders, 1965 Classification	138
Table	3. First Admissions and Resident Patients in Mental Hospitals	139
Table	4. First Admission and Resident Patient Rates	141
Table	5. First Admission Rates to Public and Private Hospitals in U.S. and U.K.	142
Table	6. Changes in Suicide Death Rate	143
Table	7. Depression and Suicide Rates	143
Table	8. Suicide Deaths in Manic-Depressive Disease	144
Table	9. First Admission Rates by Nativity	145
Table	10. First Admission Rates by Social Class	145
Table	11. Sex Distribution of Manic-Depressives and Schizophrenics by Marital Status	146
Table	12. Heterogeneous Twin Sibship Data	147
Table	13. Tuberculosis in Twin-Index Families	148
Figure	1. Suicide Rates, United States, 1900–64	149
Figure	2. Suicide Rates by Color, Sex, and Age, 1964	150
Figure	3. First Admission Rates for Functional Psychotic Disorders by Marital Status	151

THE EPIDEMIOLOGY OF
DEPRESSION

I

BASIC CONSIDERATIONS

Depression is a mood, a symptom, a syndrome, and a disease entity. As Greenacre (111) says: "Depression as a symptom is as ubiquitous as life itself, and, in a mild degree, appears 'naturally' as a reaction to loss which need hardly be questioned." When, then, is depression pathological? "It is certainly the intensity, the excessive duration and the domination of the organism by the affect, rather than its occurrence, which is pathological."

Although the difference between sadness and melancholia is, therefore, in many ways a matter of degree, depression in the psychiatric sense is also regarded as a qualitative deviation from the norm. A most compelling account of the quality of some of the differences is offered by William James (146), ". . . there is a pitch of unhappiness so great that the goods of nature may be entirely forgotten, and all sentiment of their existence vanish from the mental field. For this extremity of pessimism to be reached, something more is needed than observation of life and reflection upon death. The individual must in his own person become the prey of a pathological melancholy . . . . Such sensitiveness and susceptibility to mental pain is a rare occurrence where the nervous constitution is entirely normal; one seldom finds it in a healthy subject even where he is the victim of the most atrocious cruelties of outward fortune . . . it is positive and active anguish, a sort of psychical neuralgia wholly unknown to healthy life."

Historical Background

The historical reviews of Lewis (192), Whitwell (348), and Zilboorg (356) offer rich material on depression. Man has probably always known depression. The biblical story of King Saul (ca. 1033 B.C.) presents a quite detailed clinical account of what appears to be recurrent depression, with homicidal attempts and final suicide (348). The state of melancholia, and the word (meaning black bile), had its recorded beginning in western medicine with Hippocrates (ca. 460-357 B.C.). Melancholia was believed by Aretaeus of Cappadocia (ca. 90 A.D.) to be the beginning and even part of the disorder called "mania," an ancient foreshadowing of the manic-depressive concept.

Over time, there have been many changes of meaning attached to the word "melancholia" and fluctuating impressions of its relation to or lack of connection with mania. For example, in the eighteenth century, a distinction was made between "true" and "false" melancholia. True melancholia was considered to be bound up with a lasting sad mood and false melancholia with indifference or cheerfulness; raging melancholy was the highest form, approaching mania.

In the midst of much ferment in Europe about nosology, Zeller proposed in 1840 that all mental disease should be divided into two groups, one characterized by the dominance of affective states, and the other by disorders of ideation and will, but he maintained that in the majority of cases the first group precedes the second and, further, that there is a succession of states which can go on to complete disintegration of psychic life— the *Einheitspsychose,* the unitary concept of mental disease. Griesinger accepted the view of two fundamental states of mental abnormalities, the affective or emotional, and the ideational, and believed that most mental diseases began with depression, and that schizophrenia in its earlier stages was one of the affective disorders.

Falret, in 1851, drew attention to the differences between ordinary melancholia and the periodic variety, *la folie circulaire.* He pointed out the remissions and paroxysms, the increasing duration of each attack with advancing years, the rarity of "continuous insanity" as an ultimate outcome, the curability of its attacks but not its essence, its intermittent rather than periodic nature, the regular sequence of maniacal state, melancholic state, and lucid interval of varying duration, the possible precipitation of an outburst by exciting causes, its strongly hereditary character, and its greater frequency among women than men. As Lewis (192) points out, Falret's influence on Kraepelin in regard to manic-depressive psychosis may safely be assumed.

Magnan, in 1882, added to the description of melancholic-manic conditions by emphasizing that the form of the attack may be extremely variable, that the most unexpected combinations of mania and melancholia may be seen in the same patient, and that it is the recurrence of the attacks, whatever their form, that is the most important consideration in prognosis. Kahlbaum used the word "melancholia" for initial or transitory melancholy, a stage in the development of mental disease; he suggested "dysthymia," a term used by Hippocrates, for stable or definitive melancholy (melancholia in the modern sense of a disease rather than a morbid phase). The relation between melancholia and mental disease was described by Hecker as that between coryza and measles—the former may be an initial stage of the latter, or an independent disorder. Hecker also described the frequency of anxiety attacks in "genuine melancholia," and the features of melancholia, such as rigidity and stereotypy, which precede catatonic states.

Kraepelin's work ushered in the modern period of psychiatry with its influential nosologic principles and its insistence on the identity of causal factors, course and outcome, as the criteria of a mental disease. The unitary concept of mental disease was abandoned, and manic-depressive insanity and dementia praecox became the dominant subdivisions. In the fifth edition of his book, in 1896, Kraepelin divided all insanities into acquired disorders and those arising from morbid predisposition. Among the acquired disorders, melancholia is described as an insanity of the involutional period; among the disorders arising from a morbid predisposition, periodic insanity is given as one of the constitutional mental disorders. In "periodic insanity," manic, circular, and depressive forms are described. The independence of melancholia of the involutional period was contested by Talbitzer, Dreyfus, Hoch, and others; this finally led to modifications in Kraepelin's later works. But to this day the issue is unresolved. Bonhoeffer, and then Moebius, described exogenous types of reactions and divided mental diseases into two large classes of exogenous and endogenous diseases, which Kraepelin accepted.

In Zilboorg's interpretative book (356) there are fascinating accounts of the bewildering proliferation of classification schemes for the mental disorders, including the depressive states. At one point he notes that classificatory ambitions became so conspicuous that the composer Berlioz was prompted to remark that after completion of his studies "a rhetorician writes a tragedy and a psychiatrist a classification."

The concept of "personality illnesses" as developed by Heinroth in 1810 and Feuchtersleben in 1845 was discarded after the middle of the nineteenth century, and psychiatric illnesses were considered to be essentially diseases of the brain. The interest of psychiatrists, following the trend of German medicine, turned to postmortem pathology. Little attention was paid to the many personality disorders that were not serious enough to require hospital admission. Psychosis, insanity, and *folie* carried the connotation of committability. The distinction between psychoses and neuroses was to some extent a product of the nineteenth century, when the disorders which had anxiety or compulsion as the chief clinical feature were gradually delimited from those of "hereditary alienation" or "degeneration." The occurrence of "neurotic" symptoms in the course of melancholia had long been recognized, but the nosologic independence of "neuroses" was attained in this century (192).

Adolph Meyer, the dominant figure in American psychiatry between 1900 and World War II, developed a psychobiologic concept of *reaction types,* rather than disease entities, out of his dynamic-genetic interpretations. With regard to melancholia, he felt the term should be abandoned and in its place the term *depression* used, with distinctions made according to etiology, the symptom-complex, the course of the disease, and the outcome. His psychobiology prepared the way for the introduction of social science and psychoanalytic concepts.

With the advent of psychoanalytic theory and work in the early twentieth century, a new approach to depression was adopted. Abraham's paper in 1911 was followed by Freud's classic report on mourning and melancholia and then many others. The psychological insights into the development of depression, the fixation points in the development of the libido, the factors influencing the "choice of neurosis," and the dynamic connection between mania and melancholia have enriched concepts of depression but, like other views, have not achieved universal agreement or acceptance. When the psychoneuroses became increasingly important in the twentieth century, the impression developed that the ambulatory psychoneuroses were benign and the hospital-treated psychoses malignant, and that psychoneuroses became more intelligible through dynamic psychiatry while psychoses could not be so understood (68).

As to prevailing views on diagnosis and classification, Hoch and Zubin (134) noted that diagnostic systems still suffer from the Kraepelinian idea that psychiatric illnesses should be differentiated from each other on the basis of outcome. Although Kraepelin's basic theory that disorders that led to deterioration were a part of dementia praecox and those that did not should be classified as manic-depressive psychoses is no longer believed, there are related concepts which remain, such as the differentiation of one type of disorder from another on the basis of the degree of response to therapy.

Definitions

Although it is not possible to present definitions or concepts which can be generally agreed upon, an attempt will be made to describe some of the terms that are pertinent to a consideration of the epidemiology of mental disorders generally, and depressive states in particular. Depressive symptoms not regarded as pathologic will be considered separately, as will those associated with physical disorders or with other mental disorders. The depressive conditions of pathologic proportions with which this review is principally concerned are those which are identified *primarily* by the prominence of mood disturbances, not attributable to physical disorders; that is, the group of conditions of presumed psychogenic origin comprising the affective types of mental disorders.

First, there is the question of type of psychogenic disorder, that is, psychosis, psychoneurosis, or personality disorder, and then there is the question of type of depressive disturbance. The following descriptions of *types of mental disorders* are taken from the *Diagnostic and Statistical Manual, Mental Disorders,* prepared by the American Psychiatric Association in 1952 (6). A new edition is in preparation for publication in mid-1968, but preliminary drafts do not suggest major revisions in definitions.

> *Psychosis,* or psychotic disorder, is characterized by a varying degree of personality disintegration and failure to test and evaluate correctly external reality in various spheres. In addition, individuals with such disorders fail in their ability to relate themselves effectively to other people or to their own work.
>
> *Psychoneurosis,* or psychoneurotic disorder, has as its chief characteristic "anxiety" which may be directly felt and expressed or which may be unconsciously and automatically controlled by the utilization of various psychological defense mechanisms (depression, conversion, displacement, etc.). In contrast to those with psychoses, persons with psychoneurotic disorders do not exhibit gross distortion or falsification of external reality (delusions, hallucinations, illusions) and they do not present gross disorganization of the personality. . . . Special stress may bring about acute symptomatic expression of such disorders. . . . The various ways in which the person attempts to handle this anxiety result in the various types of neurotic reactions.
>
> *Personality disorder* is characterized by developmental defects or pathological trends in the personality structure, with minimal subjective anxiety, and little or no sense of distress. In most instances, the disorder is manifested by a lifelong pattern of action or behavior, rather than by mental or emotional symptoms. The personality pattern disturbances are considered deep-seated disturbances and sociopathic personality disturbances under stress

may at times regress to a lower level of personality organization and function without development of psychosis.

Arieti (8) has pointed out some of the differences between psychosis of a psychogenic or "functional" nature and psychoneurosis. He believes the term psychosis indicates not only actual or potential severity of the disorder (which may be true of some of the psychoneuroses) but also acceptance by the individual of the psychopathologic way of living: of relating to people and interpreting the world. The psychotic does not fight his disorder, as does the psychoneurotic, but lives in it. In this particular respect, he resembles persons with character neuroses who do not even know of the pathologic nature of their difficulties.

Redlich and Freedman (272) state that these time-honored concepts and terms, psychosis and neurosis, have been so universally accepted that realization of the difficulty of defining them has been lost. They think "the sharp boundary between neurosis and psychosis is undoubtedly spurious" and wonder why we have clung to these terms so tenaciously. "The ungratifying task" of defining neurosis and psychosis may be avoided by simply describing subcategories (136).

The concept of neurosis has been questioned as it differs from psychosis, and also as a specific disease entity in its own right; in Rennie's view it is a method of reacting (277). Some psychiatrists see normality, neurosis, and psychosis as a continuum of behavioral states; others, even though they question the distinction between neurosis and psychosis, believe the characteristics of severe psychosis suggest a discontinuity. The unitary concept of mental disease, still another approach, views all mental illness as a failure of adaptation to stresses, varying in intensity but not in essential character. Karl Menninger (224) believes that neurosis and psychosis are two stages in a five-step continuum of "dyscontrol" from nervousness to malignant anxiety and death.

DEFINITIONS

Turning now to *types of depressive states,* we find again a variety of perceptions and terms. In addition, the planned revision of the *Diagnostic and Statistical Manual, Mental Disorders* of the American Psychiatric Association will include some changes in this area which are designed to enhance international comparability. The following list of terms and definitions, therefore, is presented as a compilation of concepts in the field, without reference to a specific source or nomenclature. It includes designations which have been used in epidemiologic studies.

Types of Depressive Disorders

Affective disorders is a term applied to a group of mental disorders with a primary disturbance of affect, or mood, from which all other symptoms seem more or less directly derived. It is for all practical purposes synonymous with depressive disorders.

Manic-depressive psychosis is marked by severe mood swings from cheerfulness to sadness and a tendency to remission and recurrence. Subtypes depending on the outstanding feature, such as manic, depressed, mixed, or circular types can be described.

Involutional psychosis or involutional melancholia is most commonly characterized by depression occurring in the involutional period not attributed to a previous mood disorder.

Reactive depressive psychosis or psychotic depressive reaction is characterized by a severe depressive mood which is a reaction to some environmental precipitating factor.

Endogenous depression or endogenous psychosis is a term used for depressive psychosis presumed to be heredito-constitutional in nature and unrelated to external causes. Involutional melancholia and manic-depressive psychosis are considered to be endogenous by those who make this distinction.

Exogenous depression or exogenous psychosis is the type of psychosis which appears to develop out of traumatic environmental events. Reactive depressive psychosis would be classed in this group.

Depressive neurosis, or reactive depression, or depressive reaction, or depressive psychoneurosis, is a neurosis in which anxiety is allayed and partially relieved by depression and self-depreciation. It is precipitated by a current situation, frequently a loss of love object or possession.

Affective (cyclothymic) personality disorder is characterized by proneness to periods of depression and elation of a degree short of an affective psychosis. The mood variations appear to be stimulated by internal factors since they are not readily accounted for by external events or circumstances.

Schizo-affective psychosis is characterized by a mixture of schizophrenic and affective symptoms. The mental content may be predominantly schizophrenic with pronounced elation or depression, or there may be marked affective changes with schizophrenia-like thinking or bizarre behavior.

Psychogenic psychosis is a term used principally in Scandinavia for reactive psychoses of various types. Psychogenic depressive psychosis may be similar to psychotic depressive reaction or schizo-affective psychosis.

The distinction between an endogenous and exogenous type of psychosis is made in many European countries. In the United States, however, the classification is no longer acceptable to the majority of psychiatrists, according to Arieti. Aubrey Lewis, who has never accepted the distinction, offered some pointed comments in a general review of depressive conditions at a symposium in Cambridge, England, in 1959 (195). He related that a sociologist had said the history of *his* subject was "a graveyard of false dichotomies: nature versus nurture, society versus individual, theory versus research, ideas versus action, case method versus statistics." In remarking on the obvious similarity to the field of psychiatry, and to the psychiatry of depression, Lewis noted that in psychiatry these dichotomies had not yet reached the graveyard. He emphasized, as Whitehorn has in this country, "that it is rash to dogmatize about the possibility of differentiating between endogenous, psychogenic, typical, reactive, vital, degenerative constitutional, schizo-affective and other varieties of depressive illness."

CLASSIFICATION

Moriyama (231) has called classification the orderly arrangement of facts so that generalizations can be made from the data at hand, and he has properly described this as a fundamental process in the study of the natural history of disease. He has also drawn attention to the fact that a classificatory system, to be useful, must be dynamic in order to reflect changes in knowledge and practice.

In the general field of health, the *International Classification of Diseases,* originally entitled the *International List of Causes of Death* in 1900, has been periodically revised and broadened. Since 1948, when the classification was first extended to meet the needs of morbidity statistics, it has been revised twice. The latest, eighth, revision went into effect on January 1, 1968, for the compilation of international morbidity and mortality statistics. Major modifications have been made in several sections, including Section V, which deals with the mental disorders. Seemingly irreconcilable differences in psychiatric concepts and diagnostic practices were settled by conference, with the result that the new revision, although an improvement over the earlier one in a number of respects, is not really satisfactory to psychiatrists in the United States and many other countries in which it will be used. The affective disorders were among the areas that were particularly resistant to resolution.

The difficulties of establishing a general morbidity classification that has universal acceptance are great indeed, but relatively simple when compared with the problems surrounding the mental disorders. Stengel was commissioned by the World Health Organization Expert Committee on Mental Health to undertake a survey of existing classifications and to look into the problems of an international psychiatric classification. In his comprehensive report of 1960 (323), he reviewed historical developments in psychiatric classification and presented critiques and examples of the varying diagnostic classification systems from the United States, Canada, France, Germany, the Netherlands, Denmark, the U.S.S.R., and Japan.

The chaotic state of the classifications in use for clinical and statistical purposes was not wholly warranted by incomplete knowledge of mental disorders, in his opinion, and the situation was capable of improvement. He argued persuasively for the development of operational definitions in psychiatry, believing that many of the nosologic concepts were in reality operational definitions and suggesting that this would not be readily admitted by many psychiatrists who have the idea that our diagnostic concepts stand for biologic realities. He noted that in recent years the epidemiologic approach has been used to an increasing degree and emphasized the need for a common basic terminology and classification, if this approach is to be fruitfully employed. Lin (200) has described the WHO program for standardization of psychiatric diagnosis.

Sixteen years ago, in the United States, the American Psychiatric Association (APA) issued its first *Diagnostic and Statistical Manual, Mental Disorders,* in an effort to bring greater uniformity to the use of diagnostic terms and criteria in this country. (This followed earlier manuals published by the National Committee of Mental Hygiene in collaboration with the APA.) The diagnostic classification in this 1952 manual has been used widely in mental hospitals, outpatient clinics, and other psychiatric facilities in the United States for recording diagnostic data in patients' records, statistical reporting, and statistical tabulations of diagnosis in official published reports, as pointed out by Kramer (171). The APA classification of mental disorders also

CLASSIFICATION

constitutes the Psychobiologic Unit of the Standard Nomenclature of Diseases (261), which is the American Medical Association's standard that is used in all general hospitals in the United States for recording diagnostic data. In this way, the definitions in the APA Manual have also provided basic criteria and guidelines for use in the psychiatric departments of general hospitals and among practicing psychiatrists.

For the purposes of this review, all depressive disorders of presumed psychogenic origin, as classified in the 1952 APA *Manual* and in current use in this country, have been brought together and listed, with their appropriate code numbers from the relevant *International Classification of Diseases* (seventh revision, 1955), in Appendix Table 1.

The APA is preparing a revised Manual (DSM-II) to follow the Eighth Revision, 1968, of the *International Classification of Diseases* (ICD), in accordance with the suggestion of the World Health Organization that each country develop its own glossary for mental disorders. Preliminary drafts of the American revision indicate a significant change in the grouping of affective disorders, in line with the new international revision. The affective disorders (psychoses) are to be separated on what appears to be an endogenous-exogenous type of axis. Reactive depressive psychosis (the result of some life experience) would be taken out of the group of affective psychoses (primary mood disorders) and put under "other psychoses," while involutional melancholia, presently under a separate heading, would be placed under affective psychoses, together with the various types of manic-depressive psychosis.*

It is expected that the new manual will have even wider circulation than the extensively used original edition, because of the

---

* American Psychiatric Association: *Diagnostic and Statistical Manual of Mental Disorders,* 2nd Ed. Washington, D.C.: American Psychiatric Association, 1968.

expansion of psychiatric work in general hospitals, court consultations, industrial health services, and private office practice.

Since there is great variation among classifications in the countries that have contributed to epidemiologic information about the depressive disorders, there is little to be gained by outlining other schemes. The classification of depressive disorders in the new Eighth Revision of the ICD is presented in Appendix Table 2.

Diagnosis

The diagnosis of depression is still essentially a clinical process. There are no established criteria or objective procedures upon which there is phenomenologic, behavioral, or psychodynamic agreement. The recognition of depression results from inspection, history, interview, and empathy.

The phenomena of depression have been described by Lehmann (179) as observable and nonobservable: the observable include behavioral, autonomic, and psychologic symptoms; the nonobservable, the cerebral metabolic, and the psychodynamic. The symptoms characteristic of most types of pathologic depression are listed by Lehmann as follows: anorexia or overeating; weight loss or gain; insomnia (early waking) or excessive somnolence; frequent crying; feelings of guilt; inadequacy or deprivation; suicidal thoughts and attempts; fatigue and listlessness; inability to concentrate; decreased mental productivity; decreased sexual libido; inability to enjoy usual pleasures; and aggravation of any existing physical pathology. Clinical typing is sometimes used to describe the character of the depression, such as pathologic or normal, psychotic or neurotic, typical or atypical, retarded or agitated, endogenous or reactive. In the psychodynamic approach to diagnosis, the emphasis is not put on the symptoms but on the struggle between instinctive drives and defenses within the structure of the personality; that is, the unconscious psychologic elements behind the depressive behavior.

Manic-depressive psychosis, the major nosologic category and the only type of affective disorder in which mania is viewed as a component of the depressive process, is classically characterized by severe mood swings, with a tendency to remission and subsequent recurrence. In the manic episodes of euphoria, flight of ideas, overtalkativeness, and increased motor activity, the symptoms may vary in intensity from hypomanic to delirious mania. In the depressive periods, there may be uneasiness, apprehension, and agitation, or mental and motor retardation and inhibition up to the point of stupor. Any combination of manic and depressive episodes may occur, and there is a strong tendency toward recurrence.

Redlich and Freedman state that the diagnosis of all cyclic manic-depressive disorders is based on four considerations: (1) there must be a distinct and marked phasic disturbance of affect without accompanying cerebral pathology and without intellectual deterioration and personality disintegration; (2) the attacks must be well defined; neither very short periods of elation or depression nor lifelong depression or euphoria are characteristic; (3) the presence of other manic-depressive and cyclothymic persons in the family is considered of diagnostic value, even though we cannot distinguish between genetic and psychosocial transmission of behavioral symptoms; and (4) precipitating psychogenic factors are not conspicuous.

Bellak in 1952 offered a classic descriptive scheme of the manic-depressive psychoses in a book on the subject: "not because of particular validity but because, for historical reasons, it belongs in the kind of volume here presented" (21). More recently, Grinker and associates have noted the inexact nature of the diagnosis and deplored the fact that relatively little has been added to descriptions since antiquity (116).

Although it has been observed increasingly in recent years that the presenting clinical picture in depressive states has undergone considerable change (124, 128, 249), that depressives do not fit many of the older descriptions (96, 102, 328), and that mania is an infrequent component of "manic-depressive" disease (64, 116), the continued use of the term as the predominant category for depressive illness is still widespread. Currently, the infrequent cases of the circular type of manic-depressive disease, in which there is alternating mania and depression, appear to fit the designation most closely.

Differential Diagnosis

The detection of depressions is sometimes extremely difficult, particularly in the early stages or when there are masking signs of somatic complaints which are the presenting features. In the aged there are notable problems in detecting depression and in distinguishing affective disturbances from arteriosclerotic or senile disorders (99). The importance and unique significance of recognizing depression has been universally emphasized because of the potential risk of suicide.

The differential diagnosis between manic-depressive psychosis and schizophrenia may not be simple, particularly if, as Bellak has noted, a schizophrenic still has relatively good affect and rapport and maintains fairly good emotional contacts with others, despite intermittent primary thought disturbances. Lewis and Piotroski (196) have said that the problem of the correct diagnosis of manic-depressive psychosis is associated with that of early recognition of schizophrenia, and Bleuler stated firmly in 1924 (27) that the diagnosis of manic-depressive psychosis can be made only by elimination (of schizophrenia). A recent study by Beck (18) of thought disorder in depressed patients in psychotherapy has led him to suggest that the affective disturbance may be secondary to the thinking disorder, rather than the other way around as is commonly believed.

Reliability of Diagnosis

Accuracy of diagnosis can be determined by repeatability, sensitivity, and specificity. *Repeatability,* which is precision, is the ability to obtain the same results on repeated trials. It is the simplest of the attributes of diagnostic accuracy to attain. Although it is an essential attribute of accuracy, the converse, of course, is not true; there may be reproducibility without accuracy. *Sensitivity* is the capacity to obtain a positive result in persons who have the condition which a given procedure is designed to detect; *specificity* is the capacity to give a negative result in persons who do not have the condition. Sensitivity, which minimizes false negatives, and specificity, which minimizes false positives, can be studied only in relation to a true diagnosis. Generally, however, it is not possible to establish an absolutely true diagnosis, but reasonable assumptions can be made.

In the field of mental disorders, it is still very difficult to fulfill the first and simplest requirement, to achieve a reproducible diagnosis. That this is not unique to the mental field, however, is attested to by many examples of observer error, such as in chest x-ray readings (26) and the presence or absence of tonsils (16). A revealing clinical example regarding the detection of clubbing of the fingers was offered by Pyke in 1954 (268). He studied the agreement of sixteen observers on the presence or absence of finger clubbing in twelve patients, both by direct examination and by examination of photographs of a finger. The sixteen observers defined finger clubbing in fourteen different ways, and the results of their *direct* examinations varied from unanimity to equal division. They were less decisive in their findings, however, when they observed *photographs* of the same fingers. "Two patients, blue, breathless and with severe pulmonary heart-disease, were so much more often thought to have clubbed fingers when examined at the bedside than by photography that conscious or unconscious bias was thought to have influenced the diagnosis." Bernard Shaw expressed this eternal dilemma in the following way: "There is no harder scientific fact in the world than the fact that belief can be produced in practically unlimited quantity and intensity, without observation or reasoning, or even in defiance of both, by the simple desire to believe founded on a strong interest in believing .... Doctors are no more proof against such illusions than other men" (303).

Observer variability, patient variation, interaction between subject and observer, and standardization of diagnostic techniques are important methodologic issues in both clinical and epidemiologic investigation (104, 139, 140). Beck and colleagues (19) have presented a careful review of some of the clinical studies of reliability of psychiatric diagnoses; and Blum (28) has extensively reviewed the methods and problems of case identification in psychiatric epidemiology. A recent report by the Group for the Advancement of Psychiatry on the assessment of change in psychiatric research (118) offers a critical analysis of many of these issues. To be presented here are a few examples which include reference to the diagnosis of affective disorders.

Babigian and associates (13) used the psychiatric case register in Monroe County, New York State, to study diagnostic consistency and change in a large follow-up study of 1,215 patients reported to the register over a two-year period, 1961 and 1962. This permitted them to study hospital patients, outpatients, and private practice patients who had had the first psychiatric contact in their lifetime and who moved from service to service. Change in diagnosis was recorded in three patterns: psychosis to nonpsychosis; nonpsychosis to psychosis; and between categories of psychosis. In two-thirds of the cases involving change of diagnosis, the change was from nonpsychosis to psychosis as a patient moved *from private practice* to another service. For the other services, there was a fairly equal change from nonpsychosis to psychosis and the reverse, with minimal change between categories of psychosis. These findings suggested that the role of the psychiatrist, the setting in which the patient is seen, and the social class of the patient have considerable influence on diagnostic perception.

Whether the service was diagnostic or therapeutic, however, appeared to play a more important role than the social class of the patient. Among patients seen in *private* practice for *diagnostic* purposes, there was 73 per cent diagnostic agreement, with 19 per cent change from nonpsychosis to psychosis; for those seen privately for treatment, however, there was only 60 per cent diagnostic agreement and there was 24 per cent change from nonpsychosis to psychosis. The time lapses between contacts did not appear to be a significant factor in diagnostic consistency.

Although the over-all rate of diagnostic agreement was found to be 79 per cent, this rate was greatly influenced by the high rate of consistency (92 per cent) for the chronic brain syndrome and the low rate (46 per cent) for the affective psychosis group. The very low rate of 46 per cent for affective psychosis was heavily influenced by diagnostic disagreement in the age group 45-65, produced largely by inconsistency in judging the severity of depression; that is, marked disagreement in distinguishing psychotic from nonpsychotic states. The need for clarification of the diagnostic criteria and subgroups for the affective disorders was emphasized, particularly because depressive symptomatology is frequently missed or overlooked, especially in the aged. It was a surprising finding that, for schizophrenia, the level of diagnostic consistency was considerably higher, 70 per cent, and high enough to warrant the continued use of this category, in the opinion of the investigators.

Pasamanick and co-workers (257), in an analysis of the final diagnosis given each of 538 voluntary, female, first admissions during a two-year period at a short-term, intensive therapy, teaching hospital unit in Columbus, Ohio, found that variations in diagnosis made by psychiatrists on three separate wards were relatively slight for affective disorders, but very considerable for schizophrenia, psychoneurosis, and character disorders. The differences were attributed to the orientation of the individual psychiatrists and to changes in ward administration. It was thought that a psychoanalytic orientation affected diagnostic consistency unfavorably in schizophrenia, neurosis, and character disorder, and did not so influence the affective disorder group because the diagnoses were based on much firmer and clearer symptom pictures.

When each of 426 patients admitted to a state mental hospital in Connecticut during a six-month period was diagnosed independently by two psychiatrists, a resident and a senior psychiatrist whose diagnosis was considered "official," the poorest level of consistency among all psychoses was reported for the affective disorders. For affective psychosis there was only 35 per cent agreement; for schizophrenia, 51 per cent agreement; and for involutional psychosis, which was classed separately, the diagnosis was concordant in 57 per cent of the cases (299).

Clausen and Kohn (49) examined consistency of diagnosis for all patients from one county who were admitted to Maryland hospitals on more than one occasion during a twelve-year period. They postulated that, although patients do change and changed diagnoses would reflect changes in behavior, a comparison of the experience of patients who returned to the *same* hospital with those who entered *another* hospital would yield a rough estimate of consistency, since there should be no difference if diagnoses were consistent from hospital to hospital. This was not the case, and they found considerably less consistency on admission to another hospital (17 per cent) than on readmission to the same hospital (58 per cent). Further analysis showed that there was greater consistency in re-diagnosis of schizophrenia than in that of manic-depressive psychosis.

Brooke (33), in a cohort study of the first admissions to designated mental hospitals in England and Wales during 1954 and 1955, identified 293 patients with four hospital admissions in the two-year period. She found that even when the patient returned each time to the same hospital, 41 per cent received two different diagnoses, 16 per cent had three, and 2 per cent had four. This group was studied in further detail by Cooper (59), who investigated the reasons for changed diagnosis in 200 of the patients for whom usable records were available. Case notes were borrowed from the mental hospitals and a "standard diagnosis" was made by one psychiatrist. By regrouping the hospital diagnoses by "standard diagnosis" and then again according to *International Classification of Diseases* categories, the number of patients with the same diagnosis during the four admissions increased by this two-step process from 37 to 54 per cent and up to 81 per cent. This shift was particularly marked for the affective group, which was designated as including all varieties of manic-depressive psychosis, involutional melancholia, and neurotic depressive reaction.

Of the thirty-two patients for whom there was clear evidence in the case notes of a marked change in *clinical* state, only three patients, about 10 per cent, were judged to have had an actual change between depression and schizophrenia. Seventeen of the group had a final diagnosis of schizophrenia and most of these were of the pattern "depression with paranoid features" becoming "paranoid schizophrenia," which agreed well with the clinical impressions of schizophrenic features mentioned in the subsidiary diagnoses. The pattern of an earlier *subsidiary* diagnosis becoming the later *final* diagnosis applied, in fact, to twenty out of the total thirty-two patients. A subgroup of six patients had abnormal personalities, often with complex and changing mixtures of symptoms, and were given diagnostic labels such as "abnormal personality" or "mentally deficient" to schizophrenia, or "unstable" or "vulnerable personality" to affective illness.

The suggestion was very strong that the majority of the frequent changes in mental hospital records are not due to major changes in the clinical state of the patients but are primarily artifacts of the diagnostic and recording procedures. There was a significant relationship between the coincidence of a change in doctor with changes in diagnosis. The author concludes that the actual original clinical phenomena must be elicited and immediately recorded in a standardized manner, before hospital statistics which will give reliable information about the clinical state of patients can be obtained. He notes also that this procedure should help remove one of the "startling curiosities" in international comparisons, that of a fourteen-fold difference in hospital admission rates for "manic-depressive psychosis" between England and Wales, and the United States, to which Kramer (170) has drawn attention.

In her three-year study of mental illness in London hospitals, Norris (242) found that over two-thirds of the patients who received the diagnosis of manic-depressive psychosis (or of schizophrenia) in observation units received the same diagnosis when admitted to the receiving mental hospitals. Because the two observation units under study were very similar with respect to the proportion of discordant initial and ultimate diagnoses, this suggested that the discordancy was due not so much to differences between psychiatrists as to differences in the clinical features exhibited by psychiatric disorders at different stages of the disease.

Beck (20) and Ward and co-workers (343) undertook a study of randomly drawn new referrals to the *outpatient* service of the Philadelphia General Hospital and the Hospital of the University of Pennsylvania, designed to minimize factors that would artificially influence the rate of concordance. The 153 patients were examined independently by paired psychiatrists who were experienced and board-certified, and who agreed in advance on the diagnostic criteria to be used, as well as on a set of 22 indices for assessing the depth of depression. The highest degree of agreement obtained was for the diagnosis of neurotic depressive reaction, 63 per cent. This was followed by 55 per cent for anxiety reaction, 54 per cent for sociopathic disturbance, and 53 per cent for schizophrenic reaction. Comparison of only the major divisions of mental disorders, psychosis, neurosis, and character disorder, gave a concordance rate of 70 per cent. The agreement on the depth of depression was good, but even better when there was matching on the dimensions of specific sign and symptom clusters, irrespective of nosologic category. The investigators found that when the diagnosticians gave both a preferred and an alternative diagnosis, the rate of agreement between either diagnosis of the two diagnosticians rose to 82 per cent. This suggested that the diagnosticians may have been closer in their appraisals than indicated by the scoring of only the preferred diagnoses, which yield 54 per cent agreement. In analyzing reasons for diagnostic *disagreement,* the authors concluded that 5 per cent were due to inconstancy on the part of the patient, about one-third resulted from inconstancy on the part of the observers, and almost two-thirds were charged to inadequacies of the classification system itself.

In a factor analysis study of the phenomena of depressions at the Michael Reese Hospital in Chicago, Grinker and colleagues (116) concluded that psychiatrists could rate the feelings and concerns of patients in a highly reliable way and also interpret patients' direct statements consistently, but that they could not observe behavior well and could not communicate behavioral information well to their colleagues. Whitehorn (347) does not agree that psychiatrists are poor observers; and a recent study by Katz and colleagues (158) suggests that it is in the interpretation of the affect, particularly the level of apathy, and in the perception of reality, particularly perceptual distortion, that there is the greatest need for more objective definitions in order to achieve greater diagnostic consistency. Observational scales, it is believed, have limitations in these symptom areas, and even with the clearest language, the scales do not appear adequate to solve the problem. An interesting example of disagreement in the diagnosis of manic-depressive illness is offered. When a large group of experienced and highly skilled clinical psychiatrists viewed a film of an interview and history of a seemingly straightforward case of manic-depressive psychosis of the depressed type, only about one-half diagnosed it as such. The authors speculate that there is much current reluctance, for whatever reason, to use the manic-depressive diagnosis.

In general, it appears that the clinical diagnosis of manic-depressive psychosis and other depressive conditions is made no more consistently than would occur by chance, and that observer variability is the principal element in diagnostic discordance. In some of the study situations cited and in others (92), however, it has been shown that diagnostic agreement can be appreciably improved.

Diagnostic Techniques

The direct techniques used for the identification of cases of mental disorder and of depression, for clinical or epidemiologic purposes, include: the unstructured clinical psychiatric interview, the structured psychiatric interview, the nonpsychiatric structured interview, the nonpsychiatric guided interview, psychologic tests, symptom rating scales, psychiatric symptom reports, and social adjustment and psychiatric impairment ratings. Whatever methods are used, psychiatric evaluation is the principal final step in establishing a diagnosis.

The primary diagnostic tool, the psychiatric interview, is not a standardized procedure. Attempts to structure the interview have generally had rather unsatisfactory results except for specific study purposes. Innumerable psychologic tests and rating scales have been constructed as supplements to the clinical picture, often tailored to the particular needs of an institution or a group of investigators. The advances in psychopharmacologic therapy have greatly revived interest and activity in measuring diagnostic consistency, both for the purpose of selecting patients for treatment and for evaluating the effectiveness of treatment. The *Handbook of Psychiatric Rating Scales* (208) offers a documented account of some of the principles of rating scale design and use, and contains descriptions, critiques, and levels of reliability and validity of nineteen scales reported in the literature during the years 1950-64, five of which are specifically designed for *clinical* depressions (61, 112, 116, 123, 251).

Psychologic tests for personality assessment (133) are classed as interpretive (projective) or objective (nonprojective). The best known of the projective techniques, which include the Thematic Apperception Test (TAT), Bender-Gestalt, and Word Association tests, among others, is the Rorschach inkblot test. Among the nonprojective tests (206, 358), the most familiar is the Minnesota Multiphasic Personality Inventory (MMPI). The Minnesota Multiphasic Personality Inventory-Depression (MMPI-D) (129), with its scale of sixty items, has served as a basis for many depression rating procedures. Some investigators, however, have not found it useful for measuring depression because it was not specifically designed for this purpose and its scales are based on old psychiatric nomenclature (18); others have believed it sampled only limited areas of the depression syndrome (138).

The Cornell Medical Index (CMI), a well-known "pencil and paper" general health questionnaire, appears to have validity as a measure of the presence and degree of emotional ill health, although it is of relatively little value as an indicator of specific disorders. The CMI sections on depression and anger have been used in a study of association of these symptoms and various functional somatic symptoms (2).

While many of the scales and derived indexes are helpful diagnostic aids, they are sometimes used as definitive tests. A recent report (118) has drawn attention to the common pitfall of ignoring the limitations of data and measuring devices and simply accepting results, as well as attempting to overcome inherent data and measurement deficiencies by statistical techniques and computer aids.

II

MORBIDITY

TRENDS

Historical trends and secular changes are often quite difficult to assess and puzzling to explain. Disorders change in character over time, vary in severity, present in different forms, and rise and fall. Populations also change, as do social and cultural circumstances and customs, and patterns and methods of care (232). Some of these problems, as they relate to estimating changes in frequency of mental disorders, have been discussed in a report of the Group for the Advancement of Psychiatry (117) and in earlier reports (81, 315).

The principal source of continuing information about the

trend of mental disorders has been the statistical data collected for mental hospital patients, a method initiated by Esquirol in France in the 1830's (84). These data do not reflect the total problem since they include only treated persons, and only some of them; nevertheless, they provide relatively comparable information collected over a period of time. European countries, especially the Scandinavian ones, have the longest series.

In the United States, federal efforts to secure separate enumeration of the institutionalized mentally ill began in 1850, but it was not until 1880 that the census was considered reliable (214). In that year, a unique count was made; not only were patients with mental disease in hospital counted, but patients outside of hospital were enumerated as well, through the enlisted and enthusiastic cooperation of most of the physicians of the country. Data regarding 17 per cent of the insane were based on information obtained solely from physicians (107), and 55 per cent of the total of 91,959 patients were not in hospitals or asylums at census time. The frequency for the country as a whole was 183.3 per 100,000 population.

This determined effort to enumerate the mentally ill both in and out of hospitals was abandoned, unfortunately, in 1890, when the Bureau of the Census did not again ask for physician cooperation or encourage evaluative comment. As a consequence, the 1890 census found only 30 per cent of the enumerated insane to be in the community. A special census in 1903 concerned itself only with patients in mental institutions and set the pattern for subsequent national enumerations of the mentally ill. In 1926, the Bureau of the Census started to issue annual statistics; since 1947, these statistics have been prepared and expanded by the Biometrics Branch of the National Institute of Mental Health under the direction of Morton Kramer (339). In Appendix Tables 3 and 4, the number, percentage, and rate of first admissions and resident patients, by selected diagnoses, are presented for three time periods since 1950, to show the extent of the mental disorder problem in the public hospitals and the relative contribution of each diagnostic group.

Comparable diagnostic data for hospital patients with *depressive illnesses* in the United States have been compiled for a relatively short period of time, little more than a quarter century, for the country as a whole. Kramer and colleagues (173) have shown that first admissions of persons with affective psychoses to public mental hospitals have been decreasing steadily since 1940. For the period 1950 through 1965, more detailed analyses of patients with affective psychoses including involutional melancholia show that: (*a*) the percentage distribution of first admissions has decreased from 10.1 to 6.1; (*b*) there has been a corresponding decrease in percentage of resident patients from 10.4 to 6.9; (*c*) first admission rates have declined from 7.5 to 4.7 per 100,000 population; and (*d*) resident patient rates have fallen from 35.9 to 16.8 per 100,000 population. (Appendix Table 5 shows admission trends by age and sex.) The declining proportion of first admissions and resident patients with affective psychoses in the state and county mental hospitals of the United States has been accompanied by notable increases in psychoneuroses and personality disorders. What proportions of the neuroses and personality disorders are of a depressive nature is, however, not known.

A system of annual reporting by the outpatient psychiatric clinics in the United States was initiated in 1954 by Bahn and colleagues (14) at the National Institute of Mental Health, and it has attained increasingly broad national coverage. The percentage of patients with depressive disorders, terminated* from the outpatient psychiatric clinics in the United States, was rel-

* "Terminations" rather than "admissions" are used in reference to outpatients because information on admission is often unavailable or incomplete for diagnosis and diagnostic characteristics (as well as for factors related to service).

atively steady from 1961 through 1965; it was approximately 2.5 per cent of all diagnostic groups (239). *Rates* of termination during this time period increased from 2.1 to 4.0 per 100,000 population under the age of eighteen years, and from 17.7 to 29.8 per 100,000 aged eighteen and over. Rates for psychotic depressive reactions were low, but psychoneurotic depressive reactions were importantly represented in many age-sex groups (285).

Long before reliable mental illness statistics were available for the United States as a whole, two states, Massachusetts and New York, took the lead among official state agencies in developing and analyzing such information. Goldhamer and Marshall (105) studied first admissions to mental hospitals in Massachusetts for the hundred-year period 1840–1940, and concluded that there had been no significant increase in mental disease in patients under age fifty. The rates for older persons had increased progressively during the period, but this was attributed to increased longevity and increasing difficulty in caring for senile patients at home. Dayton (65), who studied mental hospital first admission rates in Massachusetts from 1917 to 1933, found than the annual increases over this sixteen-year period were less than one quarter of one per cent.

Plunkett and Gordon (260) looked into the five leading admission diagnoses in Massachusetts at two public mental hospitals, Boston and Worcester State, and one private hospital, McLean, over a fifty-year period, at three intervals from 1900 to 1950. They were appalled to find that in the three years selected, 1900, 1925, and 1950, the five leading admission diagnoses accounted for from 42 to 72 per cent of the total, and they concluded that historical records of mental hospital admissions were of limited and dubious value. Actually, for the diagnoses that are of interest here, they are not really that bad. Figure 1 and Table 1 are adapted from Plunkett and Gordon's table to show only the percentage of those disorders that can be classed as affective disorders among the five leading admission diagnoses.

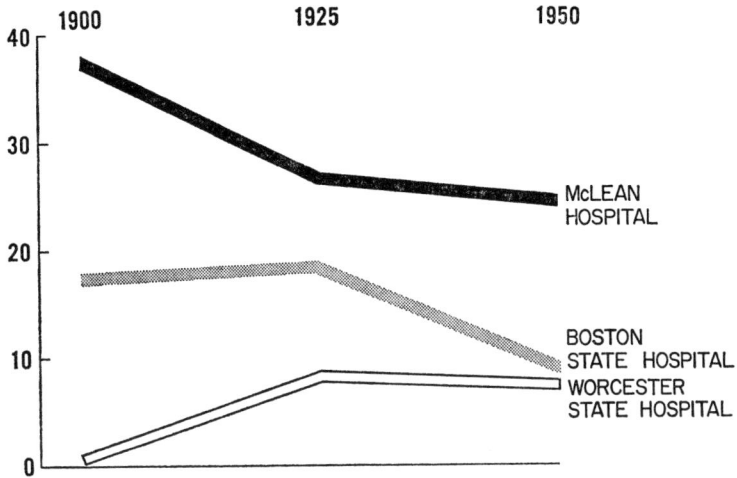

FIGURE 1.

Except for the inexplicable pattern at the Worcester State Hospital,* they show decreasing proportions of affective disorder admissions over the years, an apparent decrease in manic manifestations, and a high rate of admissions to the private hospital, all consistent with other trend findings.

For New York State, Horatio Pollock (263) adapted tabulations from the Bureau of the Census and showed that from

* Adolph Meyer introduced Kraepelin's scheme of diagnosis into the Worcester Hospital in 1896, probably the first institution outside of Kraepelin's own clinic in Heidelberg to make use of it. This change in classification may have bearing on the absence, in 1900, of any affective disorders among the five leading admission diagnoses (227, p. 150).

Table 1. AFFECTIVE DISORDERS AMONG THE FIVE LEADING DIAGNOSES ON ADMISSION TO THREE MASSACHUSETTS HOSPITALS (1900, 1925, 1950)[a]

Hospital	1900 Diagnosis	1900 Percentage	1925 Diagnosis	1925 Percentage	1950 Diagnosis	1950 Percentage
Boston State	Melancholia	10	Manic depressive psychoses	18	Manic-depressive psychoses	8
	Mania, acute	7				
Total		17		18		8
Worcester State	None in five leading diagnoses		Manic-depressive	8	Manic-depressive psychoses	7
Total				8		7
McLean	Depressive maniacal insanity	37	Manic-depressive psychoses, depressed	22	Psychoneurosis reactive depression	8
			Manic-depressive psychoses, mixed	4	Manic-depressive psychoses, mania	8
					Involutional melancholia	8
Total		37		26		24

[a] Adapted from: R. J. Plunkett and John E. Gordon: *Epidemiology and Mental Illness.* Monograph Series No. 6, Joint Commission on Mental Illness and Health. New York: Basic Books, 1960.

1880 to 1941, the rate per 100,000 population for all patient admissions to mental hospitals rose from 81.6 to 362.4. The situation was somewhat different for depressive disorders, as shown by Malzberg (214), who reported that first admissions to mental hospitals for manic-depressive psychoses increased from 1909 to about 1920. From 1933 to 1950 the rate decreased steadily, to a low of 7.1 per 100,000 population. (In Massachusetts, too, 1933 was the year in which the steady downward trend started.)

In New York State all these changes were particularly striking in regard to females. First admissions of women with manic-depressive psychosis increased until 1922, when they comprised 20.8 per cent of all first admissions; this gave an average annual rate of 12.6 per 100,000 female population. After 1922, the decrease was steady and marked; in 1950 it reached a low of 3 per cent of all admissions and a rate of only 3.0 per 100,000 female population. The decrease between 1920 and 1950 was 60 per cent for females aged fifteen years and over. Malzberg believes this was the result of an actual decrease in the number of admissions, despite a large increase in the female population.

More recent hospital data for Hagerstown, in Washington County, Maryland, show a reverse trend and illustrate some of the pitfalls of using admissions to treatment as an epidemiologic index (333). Dr. Kurt Gorwitz, Director of Statistics, Maryland State Department of Mental Hygiene, kindly prepared for me admission statistics from 1953 to 1965 which could be compared with the figures published by Clausen and Kohn (49) for the previous twelve-year period, 1940-52. In Table 2 are shown the average annual rates of first hospitalization at public and private mental hospitals, for involutional and manic-depressive psychoses (and other psychoses), among residents, aged 15 through 64 years, of the city of Hagerstown and the remainder of Washington County.

Table 2. TOTAL CASES AND AVERAGE ANNUAL RATES (PER 100,000 POPULATION AGED 15-64) OF FIRST HOSPITALIZATION FOR SPECIFIED PSYCHOSES, WASHINGTON COUNTY, MARYLAND

	1940–1952[a]					
	County Total		Hagerstown City		Remainder of County	
	No.	Rate	No.	Rate	No.	Rate
Schizophrenia	128	19.5	62	19.4	66	19.5
Involutional psychosis	57	8.7	31	9.7	26	7.7
Manic-depressive psychosis	33	5.0	17	5.3	16	4.7
Paranoia	4	0.6	2	0.6	2	0.6
Total	222	33.8	112	35.0	110	32.5
Population base	50,596		24,590		26,006	

	1953–1965[b]					
	County Total		Hagerstown City		Remainder of County	
	No.	Rate	No.	Rate	No.	Rate
Schizophrenia	314	43.1	210	71.0	104	24.1
Involutional psychosis	78	10.7	55	18.6	23	5.3
Manic-depressive psychosis	77	10.6	54	18.2	23	5.3
Paranoia	8	1.1	6	2.0	2	0.5
Total	477	65.5	325	109.8	152	35.2
Population base	56,019		22,766		33,253	

[a] From: Clausen, J. A. and Kohn, M. L.: Relation of Schizophrenia to the Social Structure of a Small City. In *Epidemiology of Mental Disorder*, B. ed. Pasamanick. Washington, D.C.: Publication No. 60, American Association for the Advancement of Science, 1959.
[b] From: Statistics Section, Maryland State Department of Mental Hygiene, Baltimore, Maryland, March, 1967. Unpublished.

The increases in first admissions from Hagerstown are startling. A combination of factors has apparently contributed to this change. Since about the middle 1950's, the attitude of patients and professionals toward hospitalization for mental illness has become more favorable. The addition of drugs to the therapeutic regimen and the greater involvement with community problems on the part of hospital and other professionals have led to increased contact with patients and former patients. The private hospital located near Hagerstown, which had just opened in 1949, is now widely used; it has a good reputation, charges reasonable rates; and evidently can be afforded by many people for the prevailing short periods of hospitalization.

It has not been possible to obtain trend data for the *manic* types of affective psychoses. The frequently voiced question "What has happened to mania?" is based on widespread clinical impressions of the steadily decreasing manifestation of mania. Along with this is the progressive replacement of the diagnosis of manic-depressive psychosis by depressive designations, both psychotic and neurotic. A few episodic observations which relate to this question are offered.

In Kraepelin's series of manic-depressive patients, 17 per cent were of the manic type and 34 per cent were of the mixed or circular type (168). Manic-depressive patients admitted to the Henry Phipps Clinic in Baltimore from 1913 to 1916 were categorized by Rennie (276) as being 8 per cent manic and about 25 per cent mixed-type. For the 1889-1928 period, Ödegaard (243) found a ratio of 3.5 depressions per mania among Norwegian-born patients in Minnesota and 2.5 depressions per mania among Norwegians hospitalized in Norway. Faris and Dunham (91) found a few more depressed types than manic types, with very few mixed forms, in the Chicago material for 1922-34. In mental hospitals in England in 1949, Norris (242) reported that 88 per cent of the manic-depressives were depressive psychotics and very few were cyclic. Of the affective psychotic patients admitted to a teaching hospital in St. Louis in 1961-62, 9 per cent were reported to have the manic form of the disease (50). In Boston a comparison of similar admissions for the three years 1945, 1955, and 1965 (287) showed the ratios of depressed to manic forms of manic-depressive psychoses to vary considerably and inconsistently; the most notable finding, however, was the marked reduction in 1955 in the number of cases diagnosed as manic-depressive psychosis and its subtypes.

In most of the community surveys in which these distinctions have been made there have been many more depressive cases than manic types, except in Formosa (199, 279), where manic-type cases predominated among the manic-depressives. It has been said that in Scandinavian and other northern European countries a predominance of depression is found, whereas in southern Europe mania is more frequent. It is not possible to substantiate the higher relative frequency of mania in the south of Europe. A report of the prevalence of mental disorders in Italy (284) notes that for the five-year period 1951-55, manic-depressive psychosis was the category of mental illness most frequently used by physicians (for 30 per cent of all mental illness in males and 32 per cent in females), but separation by subtypes was not made. In a southern area in another part of the world, the Caribbean, mania was reported to have been almost twice as frequent as depression in hospitalized patients in 1960 (290).

There is no evidence that "civilization" brings with it an increase in depression or mental disorder, despite the many persuasive impressions to the contrary. Panum (256), whose observations on a measles epidemic in the Faroe Islands (Denmark) are a classic, had the following general remarks to make about the people of the Faroes during his visit in 1846:

> Since it has been proved that the frequency of mental diseases is generally in direct proportion to civilization and its accompanying social collisions, it might be surmised that these diseases are extremely rare on the Faroes, inasmuch as civilization has certainly not attained a high degree there, and the social collisions so agitating to the mind, under the patriarchal conditions which prevail, are proportionately very few. But on the contrary, there is hardly any other country, or indeed any metropolis, in which mental diseases are so frequent in proportion to the number of people as on the Faroes. Unfortunately I am not able for the

moment to present positive statistical data in regard to this proportion; but I have been in most of the towns of the islands, and can assert that in nearly all places that are inhabited by 100 or 200 persons, one or more weak-minded persons are found; and I do not believe that I am exaggerating in assuming that at least one per cent of the Faroese are mentally weak. This fact is the more striking because the Faroese in general are endowed with excellent mental powers.

Prevalence and Incidence

The problems posed by diagnostic and classification uncertainties are considerable for epidemiology, as they are for psychiatry, although in different ways. As Sartwell (295) has said, the epidemiologist asks the question: "Does or does not this individual have the condition which I am studying?" not "What condition does this patient have?" He cannot wait for the passage of time to settle the question, as the clinician often does. Ambiguities of case specification limit the reliable use of the two measures of morbidity which together provide information about the magnitude of a problem in the population, namely: prevalence, the number of cases active at a given time (a cross-sectional measure of cases on hand); and incidence, the number of new cases developing during a stated period of time (a measure of the occurrence of cases).

Because several forms of prevalence have been used in studies of mental disorder, a brief comment on definitions may be in order. In the usual sense of the word, prevalence is *point prevalence;* that is, frequency at a given point in time, usually a day. When cases are observed during a period of time, rather than at a given time, *period prevalence* is described. The period may be specified in weeks, months, one year, or longer. *Lifetime prevalence* is a measure which includes the proportion of the population who at any time in their lives have had the condition being counted. This involves so many unassessable factors and assumptions that interpretation in terms of frequency distribution does not seem possible.

Deficiencies in knowledge, inadequacies in case-finding techniques, and lack of established mechanisms for reporting and enumeration often lead to various approximations of prevalence. Because the time of onset of many conditions, including the mental disorders, is uncertain, it is even more difficult to measure incidence directly. Approximations such as onset of symptoms, time of diagnosis, date of report, or date of first admission to hospital or other treatment are commonly used. These substitutes for incidence have varying degrees of usefulness, depending on the type of disorder, the system of care, and the completeness and consistency of the recording system.

In an effort to gauge the full dimension of the mental disorder problem, population surveys have been made in communities all over the world in large number during the past fifty years. Some of them have been directed specifically toward the study of prevalence or incidence; others have had different purposes but have yielded such information as a byproduct. The surveys seem to have followed two historical streams of development. The first, largely European, originating in Germany and later widely represented in Scandinavia, has its roots in psychiatric genetics and its interest in exploring the hereditary and constitutional mechanisms in mental disease and deficiency; its emphasis is largely on disease expectancy or incidence. The second, reflecting practice in the United States as well as other countries, is associated with social and administrative purposes, and more directly concerned with program development objectives; its emphasis is on prevalence and it often includes the "minor" mental and personality disorders with the psychoses. Lemkau, Tietze, and Cooper in 1943 (188), Strömgren in 1948 (327), and Cowie and Slater in 1959 (60) offer interesting insights into these developmental trends in the course of their reviews of many of the studies.

The genetic line of development followed growing awareness in groups concerned with human genetics that the study of families of only sick individuals was not sufficient, and that knowledge of morbidity in the general population was necessary if accurate probabilities were to be determined. Luxenburger (207) and others in Munich in the 1920's worked out techniques for population sampling, case finding and diagnosis, and statistical analysis which have been widely used, with later modifications, in genealogically oriented surveys. The techniques have also been adapted to population studies which have other objectives. In surveys of this kind, incidence is presented in terms of lifetime expectancy; that is, the chance of developing or acquiring a specific disease if the individual lives through the age period of susceptibility. The age periods of susceptibility to the principal psychoses are laid down, although they have varied in different studies; for example, twenty to fifty years has been a commonly assumed period of risk from manic-depressive psychosis. The computation of expectancies is usually made by a formula devised for this purpose by Weinberg (346) and later modified and known as Weinberg's abridged method.* When prevalence is measured in such surveys, it is generally stated in terms of lifetime prevalence. In many other types of community surveys of mental disorders, lifetime prevalence has also been used for less understandable reasons.

The number of published morbidity surveys of mental disorder is by now quite large; perhaps as many as forty have ap-

* The number of cases of the disease is the numerator (N), and the total number in the population who have passed the age of susceptibility (A) plus one-half of those who are in the age period of susceptibility (B) are in the denominator. Thus: Corrected incidence (expectancy) $=$
$$\frac{N}{A + \frac{1}{2}B} \times 100\%$$

peared (Gruenberg estimated two dozen in 1963). Various groups of them have been summarized and reviewed in different ways by Lin and Standley (201), Zubin (357), Gruenberg (119), Plunkett and Gordon (260), Mishler and Scotch (229), Taylor and Chave (331), Dohrenwend and Dohrenwend (69), Clausen (48), and others (176, 184, 353). Reviews, it seems, appear almost as frequently as surveys. Because so many of the reviews have analyzed in great detail the specifics of population sampling, case definition, method and intensity of ascertainment of cases, diagnostic reliability, and method of analysis and interpretation of findings, it seems unnecessary to go over this ground again, except to repeat that the community surveys have lacked comparability one with another. Even when the stated intention has been to make comparisons with other communities, or when a survey has followed an earlier one in precisely the same community, or when the investigators have been trained in the same "school," there is little basis for reliable comparisons.

Most of the community surveys have been concerned with the total problem of mental disorders; some have given attention to specific diagnostic categories, especially schizophrenia; a smaller number have data for the depressions. Only a few, in the Scandinavian countries, have been particularly designed to study the depressive disorders.

In this review, the survey literature has been screened by a two-step process: first, by identifying the surveys which present findings on depressive conditions (a considerably smaller number than the total); and, second, by selecting from them the studies which, as presented or through recalculations, can be examined in terms of point and period prevalence and of some approximations of incidence. Most of the prevalence rates have been recomputed from the data and diagnostic categories available in the original publications. This procedure in no way

PREVALENCE AND INCIDENCE

changes the lack of comparability of methodologies and populations; it simply groups the surveys and expresses the findings in universally used epidemiologic terms of morbidity measurement.

Prevalence

Community Surveys: Point Prevalence. Seven studies are presented in Table 3: they report findings in terms of lifetime prevalence but distinguish between current and old cases on the census date of prevalence determination, thereby making possible the computation of estimated active prevalence rates.

The surveys were carried out between 1938 and 1960 and include the Roth and Luton (289) study in Williamson County, Tennessee, U.S.A.; the Sjörgen (309) study in a west-coast Swedish island; the Böök (30) investigation in north Sweden; the survey of Essen-Möller (86) in two rural parishes in south Sweden; the study of a cohort of the population in Iceland by Helgason (130); the investigation of the Danish island of Samsø by Sørensen and Strömgren (316); and a survey of the adult population in a district of Prague, Czechoslovakia, by Ivanys and co-workers (143).

The range of findings is enormous; it is made so by the investigations in Iceland and Samsø. These two studies, using virtually identical diagnostic criteria, obtained almost the same very high prevalence rates for depressive psychoses and neuroses. Even though they are markedly different from the other studies, this might seem a good illustration of consistency except for the fact that the Iceland study cohort population was aged sixty to sixty-two years, and the Samsø rates are based on the population aged fifteen years and over. (In Samsø, less than 10 per cent of the total population was in the sixty to sixty-five age group.) The Danish investigators have stated (241) that the Samsø proj-

Table 3. Estimates of Point (One-day) Prevalence of Depressive Disorders.[a] Selected Community Surveys, Rates per 1,000 Population

Authors	Year of Publication	Source of Data	Population Studied	Total Depressive Disorders	Psychoses Total	Manic-Depressive	Involutional	Endogenous	Psychogenic depression	Neuroses
Roth and Luton	1943	USA, Williamson Co., Tenn., Sept. 1, 1938	Total population: 24,804		0.7					1.4
Sjörgen	1948	Sweden, A:bo Island, W. Coast, Dec. 31, 1944	Total population: 8,736			0.5				
Böök	1953	Sweden, 3 parishes in North, Sept. 1, 1949	Total population: 8,981			0.2[b]				
Essen-Möller	1956	Sweden, 2 parishes in South, July 1, 1947	Total population: 2,550			2.0[c]				5.8
Helgason	1961	Iceland, July 1, 1957	Cohort born 1895–97: 3,843	38.2[d]	10.4[d,e]			5.4[d,e]	3.9[d,e]	25.5[d,e]
Sørensen and Strömgren	1961	Denmark, Samsø Island, Jan. 1, 1960	Total population: 6,447	34.4[f]				5.0[f]	2.8[f]	26.5[f]
Ivanys et al.	1964	Czechoslovakia, Prague (district 8), Dec. 31, 1960	Total adult population: 66,165			0.95[f]	0.45[f]			

[a] Estimated rates computed by author from data in the original publications.
[b] Based on two cases both with equivocal diagnosis. Böök found manic-depressive psychosis very rare.
[c] Of the five cases, three were classed as depressive psychosis and two as manic psychosis.
[d] Per 1,000 population aged 60–62 years.
[e] Includes depressive psychoses only. Cases of manic-depressive psychosis with only manic attacks or circular psychosis are excluded.
[f] Per 1,000 population fifteen years and over.

ect as a whole, including other studies, cannot be compared with any other community psychiatric project; it even differs markedly from the rest of Aarhus County, of which it is a political subdivision. Parenthetically, it may be mentioned that the same relationship obtains between the island of Martha's Vineyard, studied by Milton Mazer (218), and the state of Massachusetts, of which it is a part. Mazer visited Juel-Nielsen and others in Samsø in 1966 and learned that the two islands are quite alike in important social and demographic characteristics. Explorations are under way to try to reconcile the different diagnostic criteria, in anticipation of a possible comparative study.

Among the remaining five studies listed in Table 1, a more limited range can be found for the single category of manic-depressive psychosis. If the very low rate found by Böök in north Sweden is not considered, because Böök himself thought the two cases doubtful and noted the extreme rarity of manic-depressive psychosis in the highly inbred population that he studied, then the prevalence rates for manic-depressive psychosis are found to range from 0.5 to 2.0 per 1,000 population.

Community Surveys: Period Prevalence. Estimates of period prevalence rates in six community surveys are shown in Table 4. This is a poor grouping because the periods of investigation vary from six months to several years; the table is presented in this way in order to identify the type of prevalence measure used in some well-known surveys. The surveys were made from 1933 to 1960 by Cohen and Fairbank (52, 53) in the Eastern Health District of Baltimore, Maryland; Lemkau, Tietze, and Cooper (185, 186), also in the Eastern Health District; Eaton and Weil (80) in the Hutterite colonies in Manitoba and Alberta, Canada, and in the Dakotas of the United States; Yoo (354) in South Korea; Lin (199) in Formosa; and Leighton and co-workers (181, 137, 183) in Nova Scotia, Canada.

Table 4. ESTIMATES OF PERIOD PREVALENCE OF DEPRESSIVE DISORDERS[a]
SELECTED COMMUNITY SURVEYS, RATES PER 1,000 POPULATION

Authors	Year of Publication	Source of Data	Population Studied	Psychoses — Total	Psychoses — Manic-Depressive	Psychoses — Involutional	Psychoses — Psychotic Depression	Neuroses
Cohen and Fairbank	1938	USA, E. Health Dist., Baltimore, Md., 1 year, 1933	Total population: 56,044	0.8[b]	0.1[b]	0.1[b]	0.6[b,e]	
Lemkau, et al.	1941	USA, E. Health Dist., Baltimore, Md., 1 year, 1936	Total population: 55,129	0.9	0.7	0.1		0.3[c]
Eaton and Weil	1955	Canada and USA, 93 Hutterite colonies, 1 year, 1950–51	Total population: 8,542		0.9[d]			
Leighton, et al.	1963	Canada, "Stirling County," C. 5 years, 1952–56	Total population: 20,000	3.0[e]				72[e]
Lin	1953	China, Formosa, 6 months, 1946–48	Total population in 3 areas: 19,931		0.4			
Yoo	1961	Korea, 6 areas in South, 5 years 1956–60	Total population: 11,974		0.3			

[a] Estimated rates computed by the author from data in the original publications, except for Leighton and Yoo.
[b] Per 1,000 population aged fifteen and over.
[c] Includes reactive depression.
[d] Includes only those ill and those ill but improved at time of survey.
[e] "Current symptom patterns" described by the investigators in diagnostic terms.

Five of the studies used the diagnostic category of manic-depressive psychosis and, regardless of the period of investigation, found a prevalence rate of less than one per 1,000 population. In fact, the prevalence rate for all types of depressive psychoses—manic-depressive psychosis, involutional depression, psychotic depression, and reactive depression—when designated, remained below one per 1,000, except in the Leighton study, where the rate was 3.0 per 1,000, based on "current symptom patterns." Attention is drawn to the study of Eaton and Weil, which reported high rates of depressive disorder among the Hutterites. When the cases active at the time of the survey are separated from the recovered cases, the period prevalence rate is found to be 0.9 per 1,000 for the year, in contrast to the original reported lifetime prevalence rate of 4.6 per 1,000.

Diagnosed Cases. In Maryland, where all mental hospitals, psychiatric services in general hospitals, and outpatient clinics have reported to a central, cumulative psychiatric case register since 1961, the one-day prevalence rate, age-adjusted, on July 1, 1963, for all depressive disorders was 0.46 per 1,000 population (239). The principal diagnostic categories in the group were manic-depressive reaction (0.13) and psychoneurotic depressive reaction (0.21); psychoneuroses comprised almost one-half of the total group of depressive reactions. When admissions to psychiatric treatment for the year from July 1, 1962, to June 30, 1963, were compared with point prevalence rates, they were found to be substantially higher for total depressive reactions (0.78) and psychoneurotic reactions (0.59) and lower for all psychotic groups except psychotic depression.

Bahn and co-workers (15) recently published a comparison of admission and prevalence rates for psychiatric facilities in four areas in the United States which have central registries in various stages of development: the State of Maryland; Monroe

County, New York State; the State of Hawaii; and Tricounty, North Carolina. A report of five years' experience with the Monroe County register, which has been in operation since 1960 and is the only one to which virtually all practicing psychiatrists report, is in preparation by Gardner and colleagues.

In Denmark, there has been a central registry for treated cases in Aarhus County since January, 1958. One-year prevalence rates for 1958 were reported by Juel-Nielsen and others (150) as 3.6 for all depressions, 1.0 for endogenous depression, 1.0 for psychogenic depression, and 1.5 for depressive neurosis, per 1,000 population aged fifteen years and over. Within the past ten years, there have been numerous publications by Strömgren and the staff of the Institute of Psychiatry at Aarhus State Hospital in Risskov, Denmark, where the register has been developed for continuing psychiatric-demographic research projects in Samsø and Aarhus County (25, 151). The problems of depression have received particular attention from this group.

Medical Practitioners' Patients. Psychiatric problems manifested by people who come to nonpsychiatric physicians have been investigated more often in independent studies than as part of larger community morbidity surveys and have been done most extensively in Great Britain (271, 291). Increasing prevalences of mental disorders are found as the criteria for mental disturbance are expanded (160, 305). Most of the investigations deal with broad groups of mental disorder, with infrequent designation of depressive conditions.

Although it was not specified, depression was found to be the dominant subgroup of psychoneurotic cases in a Maryland county study (204) in which psychoneurosis was diagnosed in one-third of the nine per cent of patients considered to have a psychiatric problem when they were seen during one week in 1964. Mazer (219) found the yearly prevalence rates for all depressive disorders reported by general practitioners on the small island of Martha's Vineyard to be 7.1 for men and 16.6 for women per 1,000 population in 1966 (three of fifty-three depressed patients had psychotic depression). Taylor and Chave (331) found yearly prevalence rates among adult patients of general practitioners in two new towns near London to be about three per 1,000 for psychotic depression, between 4.0 and 6.7 for neurotic depression, and 11 to 17 for the simple depressed state. Jones and Miles (149) included a general practitioner study in their survey of mental health needs of the rural area of Anglesey in Wales and reported that mild depressions are described by a presenting anxiety or other neurotic symptom and rarely come to psychiatric treatment. When a patient is sufficiently depressed for his condition to be called depression by the general practitioner, he is in need of treatment and is generally referred for psychiatric treatment.

Depressive Symptoms in General Population Groups. A number of surveys have focused attention on the frequency distribution of symptoms of possible psychiatric significance (120, 182). The two most ambitious and best known are the Midtown Manhattan Study, conducted in New York City during 1953-54 and reported in two volumes by Srole and colleagues in 1962 (319) and Langner and Michael in 1963 (175), and the Stirling County Study, conducted in a rural area in Canada over a number of years and reported by Alexander and Dorothea Leighton and co-workers in three volumes in 1959 (181), 1960 (137), and 1963 (183).

The New York City study classified 23.6 per cent of the surveyed urban population in the depression symptom group. These respondents were considered to have a tendency toward assuming a pessimistic viewpoint toward life situations, health problems, and interpersonal relationships. Among the rural residents of Nova Scotia, Canada, 7.2 per cent made statements of a low mood and showed depressive symptoms.

In a "new town" near London, during 1954-55, Martin and colleagues (217) carried out a family health survey in which self-reported symptoms were given. Simple depression was complained of by 10 per cent of the men and 24 per cent of the women. Among men, the degree of variation with age was not very great. Among women, however, the frequency of each of four complaints increased steadily with age until 65, when it fell off sharply. It was also observed that for each of the symptoms there is a different point on the age scale at which the frequency of the complaint rises with particular steepness. For example, the frequency of "nerves" is at least doubled after the age of twenty-four; the major increase in the occurrence of depression comes ten years later; and complaints of sleeplessness rise steeply in the mid-forties. The group of four symptom-complaints, nervousness, depressed state, insomnia, and headache, was thought to represent a subclinical neurosis syndrome. This is similar to the conclusion reached by Lemkau and others (187) on the basis of findings in the 1936 Eastern Health District Survey: persons who reported themselves or were reported as being nervous were similar with respect to race, age, and sex to those diagnosed as having neurasthenia, psychoneurotic depression, and hypochondriasis.

Incidence

Community Surveys. A ten-year incidence study of mental disorder was reported by Hagnell in 1966 (121) in what he has designated the "Lundby Project." This study was a re-examination made in 1957 of the population in two adjoining rural parishes in southern Sweden that had been studied intensively by Essen-Möller and colleagues in 1947 (86, 85) when the population numbered 2,550. This is one of the very few attempts to investigate the rate at which new mental disorder develops in a community. Although there was the supposed advantage of working with a relatively stable population, it was learned that the area had changed economically and socially, had become more urbanized, and had lost more than one-fourth of its residents during the intervening ten years. Nevertheless, all original inhabitants could be accounted for and the newcomers identified.

A thorough survey was done, involving personal examinations by interview and observation and the gathering of pertinent information from official and personal sources. Regardless of their residence, each of the surviving individuals originally studied by Essen-Möller and his colleagues in 1947 was again interviewed psychiatrically by Hagnell in 1957. Hagnell's particular interest in this follow-up study was in mental illnesses as a group, rather than as diagnostic entitles, and in determining levels of impairment and the presence of possible premorbid factors in those who became ill. Essen-Möller shared in some of the interviewing at the start of the project, and also rated a number of the records. The Leightons' descriptions of degree of impairment and certainty of diagnosis were used, and the Leightons themselves served as independent raters for a random sample of the subjects. Symptom patterns were defined in diagnostic terms, much as in the procedure followed in the Stirling County survey in Nova Scotia.

Lifetime prevalence among former residents and newcomers and incidence and expectancy of mental disorder in the 1947 cohort were the morbidity measures used. The presentation of the material creates some problems in calculating the incidence of depressive disorders over the ten-year period because the symptom-patterns often do not correspond with the diagnostic categories or earlier groupings of Essen-Möller. There are also uncertainties about the base population and the number of new cases at various times during the decade.

For the 2,480 individuals with no history of depression in 1947, there were 23,521 person-years of observation during the decade (11,316 for females and 12, 205 for males) (87). First occurrences of a depression during the ten-year period numbered forty-one, of which three were psychotic (all in women), eighteen were "depression" (apparently neurotic depression). and twenty were "depression with other psychiatric symptoms" (no further description given).

There is little to compare with the frequencies for depressive illnesses, but the findings for all mental disorders of the severe type agree fairly well with other earlier investigations, according to Hagnell (121). For the purpose of studying the depressive disorders, one must express regret that Hagnell had not had the opportunity to re-examine this population at an earlier point or at several points during the decade. Depressive illnesses have a way of coming and going, with the result that a single ten-year observation period, which may have utility for the more chronic forms of mental disorder and for personality types, has more limited value for depression. It is to be hoped that the deaths that occurred during the period will be discussed in a later publication. There were ten suicides and nineteen suicide attempts (two of those who attempted suicide were dead from unstated causes). No information is given about the time of death, premorbid condition, or diagnosis, information that would have extreme relevance for the study of depressive conditions.

Diagnosed Cases. Approximations of incidence of mental disorders have most commonly been made in terms of first admissions to psychiatric treatment. Until recent years, first admission to treatment was given as first admission to a mental hospital. In Norway, hospital admission data have been used with versatility and skill for many years by Ödegaard, who believed that most mentally ill persons in his country would find their way into the hospital at some time during their lives, although hospitalization would be decidedly more complete for schizophrenia than for depressive states (245).

Table 5. SELECTED STUDIES OF FIRST ADMISSIONS TO PSYCHIATRIC TREATMENT (HOSPITAL AND OTHER) FOR DEPRESSIVE DISORDERS.
AVERAGE ANNUAL RATES PER 1,000 POPULATION

Authors	Year of Publication	Source of Data	Population Studied	Total	Psychoses Manic-Depressive	Psychoses Involutional	Psychoses Psychotic Depression	Neuroses
Faris and Dunham	1939	USA, Chicago, Ill. All state and private mental hospitals, 1922–34	Total population: 2.5 million		0.07[a]			
Malzberg	1955	USA, New York State. All public and private mental hospitals, 1949–51	Total population: over 14 million		0.07[a]	0.23[b]		
Hare	1956	England, Bristol. All public and private mental hospitals, 1949–53	Total population: ½ million		2.4			
Jaco	1960	USA, State of Texas. All public and private hospitals, and private psychiatrists,[c] 1951–52	Total population: 7.7 million		0.11	0.05		
Nat. Institute Mental Health	1967	USA, State of Maryland. All psychiatric facilities reporting to central register, 1962–63[d]	Total population: 3 million	0.18	0.08	0.02	0.08	0.59

[a] Per 1,000 population aged fifteen and over.
[b] Per 1,000 population aged thirty-five and over.
[c] Diagnosed psychosis only.
[d] Unpublished data.

During recent years, the increase in alternative methods of treatment and the expansion of sources of reporting have made it possible to determine first admissions to other types of treatment in addition to mental hospitals. In Table 5, average annual rates of first admissions to treatment, in a hospital or elsewhere, are presented from five large studies. The first three, reported between 1939 and 1956, cover only mental hospital admissions. They are the Faris and Dunham study (91) of first admissions to all state and private mental hospitals serving the city of Chicago during the twelve-year period 1922-34; the study by Malzberg (213) of first admissions to all the public and private mental hospitals in New York State during the three-year period 1949-51; and the study by Hare (127) of first admissions to all the public and private hospitals serving the city of Bristol, England, during the five-year period 1949-53. The other two investigations include other treatment sources. Jaco (144) reported on entrance into treatment, for psychosis only, at all public and private hospitals and with private psychiatrists, in the state of Texas during 1951-52; and the Biometrics Branch of the National Institute of Mental Health (239) prepared tabulations for the state of Maryland for 1962-63, the third year of operation of a central psychiatric register to which all mental hospitals, psychiatric outpatient clinics, and psychiatric services in general hospitals in the state reported.

Only the category of manic-depressive psychosis was used in the earliest study in Chicago; the average annual rate of first hospital admission was 0.07 per 1,000 population aged fifteen years and over. The New York State admission rate for all depressive psychoses was slightly higher, as is seen by the separate specification of involutional psychosis (for which the rate is based on the population aged thirty-five and over). In the Texas study, the rate for manic-depressive psychosis was 0.11 and for involutional psychosis 0.05, yielding a combined annual rate of

0.16 per 1,000 total population. The Maryland figures, which are the most recent and which offer finer diagnostic categorization, show an average rate for all depressive psychoses of 0.18 per 1,000 population; making up this total rate for psychoses are the following diagnostic categories and their respective rates: manic-depressive, 0.08; involutional, 0.02; psychotic depression, 0.08. In addition, depressive neuroses were reported at the rate of 0.59 per 1,000 total population.

In Bristol, England, the rate of first hospital admissions for manic-depressive psychosis was enormously greater than in the United States at any period: 2.4 per 1,000 population. Kramer (170) suggested that repeated observations of this large difference in hospital admission rates between the two countries (see Appendix Table 5) warranted investigation and a joint study is now in progress to compare diagnostic criteria and the process of making a diagnosis in the United States and the United Kingdom. Slater (310) in 1935 thought it very probable that there was more manic-depressive psychosis in England than in Germany or in Switzerland.

III

MORTALITY: SUICIDE

Plunkett and Gordon (260) note that a satisfactory knowledge of case fatality may give a working approximation of incidence; and with additional facts about the average duration of illness, a fair idea of prevalence may be achieved. Although mental disorders account for many illnesses, they result directly in few deaths (since general paresis has become so rare), except for suicides. Deaths, therefore, are of no value as a general index of the frequency of mental illness.

For depressive mental illness, however, it is possible to think of specific case fatality in terms of suicide. There is no psychiatric observer of depressive disorder (of any degree of severity) who does not take into account the potential for suicide (11). Muncie has said that when depression is deep, it may be assumed to be associated with suicidal preoccupation and to demand adequate protection for the patient (233). Some general trends and factors in suicide will be reviewed and then the relationships of mental disease and depressive illness to suicide will be examined.

General Trends and Factors in Suicide

Principal sources for this introductory section are Dublin's (72) important contribution to international compilation and analysis; the study by MacMahon and others (210) of the relation of suicide rates to social conditions; and reports from the National Center for Health Statistics of the U.S. Public Health Service on mortality trends from all causes (341) and suicide trends (340).

The problems of ascertainment, reporting, and assignment of deaths as suicides are enormous and practices vary greatly, not only among nations but also within each country. Appendix Table 6 is presented to show cross-national comparisons and trends in suicide rates in principal countries of the world during a recent fifty-year period. There is no consistent pattern from 1910 to 1960; there are increases, decreases, and relatively stationary rates. The highest rates tend to be reported from Austria, the lowest from Ireland.

Suicide rates in the United States, both crude and adjusted, have varied from year to year. Maximum rates have been reached during years of economic depression and low figures during war periods. Rates in recent years are similar to those at the beginning of the twentieth century (Appendix Figure 1).

An increase in the suicide rate that began in 1958 (the result, in part, of the changed classification of certain self-inflicted injuries to suicides) continued with minor fluctuations through

1965. The rate increased from 9.8 suicides per 100,000 population in 1957 (the lowest rate recorded in this century) to 10.7 during 1958, 11.0 in 1963, and 11.1 for 1965, per 100,000 (representing in 1965 a total of 21,507 suicides, approximately one per cent of deaths from all causes). Suicide has been among the twelve leading causes of death in the United States since 1954, and it is now among the first ten.

Universally, males are reported to have a higher suicide rate than females at all ages. In the United States, the total rate for males is almost three times that for females. Both the male and female rates increase with age up to about age fifty-five, after which the male rate continues to rise while the female rate declines. This pattern of divergence is characteristic for the United States and is seen in only a few other countries. In some countries, the divergence of rates may occur at a later age (England and Wales), or there may be no divergence at all, with rates for each sex continuing to increase with advancing years (France and the Netherlands), or to decrease (Finland and Sweden). In Japan, a striking pattern of bimodality has been described; in it the male and female curves remain closely parallel throughout life, peaking at twenty, dropping during the age period between thirty-five and forty-five, and then rising sharply and continuously to age eighty.

In the United States, suicide occurs more frequently in the white than in the Negro population, in a ratio of about two to one. In the northern regions of the country, however, suicide rates for Negroes up to age thirty are as high as those for white people, and the differences after age thirty-five are not as great as they are in the south. Negro males show a greater tendency to approach the rates in white persons than do Negro females (Appendix Figure 2).

It is generally found that marital status is a correlate of suicide and that married persons, especially those with children, commit suicide less often than those who have never been married or whose marriages have been broken by divorce or death. In the United States, for the period 1950-64, the suicide rate, age-adjusted, was lowest for married persons; next in rank were single persons, followed by the widowed and, finally, divorced persons, among whom the rate was highest.

In the past, urban-rural comparisons have tended to show that the larger the city the higher the suicide rate. In the United States, however, where there has been the most striking trend toward urbanization, the gap between urban and rural rates has greatly narrowed in recent years as a result of a persistent decline in suicide in the cities and little change in the rural areas. This change has not been observed in many European areas.

There is no evidence that the incidence of suicide is significantly related to climate. On the other hand, seasonal rhythms have been widely observed. In most countries suicides are more frequent not during the dark, cold, and dreary months of the year but in the springtime. In the United States the month of April nearly always has the highest daily average number of suicides, and December the lowest.

The influence of religion on the suicide rate cannot be measured very well, since religious affiliation is not tantamount to religious belief or practice. Religious attitudes may well affect the *reporting* of suicide, however, and thus influence the rate. In general, suicide mortality is lowest in countries where a large proportion of the population is Catholic; and the suicide rate among Catholics is reported as being much lower than that among Protestants living in the same country. Suicide rates were very low among the Jews of Europe in the nineteenth century but rose greatly under persecution and threat of annihilation. During recent years, in Israel and in the United States, suicide rates among Jews have returned to their original reported low levels.

Studies of the association of suicide with social and economic circumstances have yielded generally equivocal information because of the complexity of the interrelationships. In England and Wales, and in the United States, suicide has been found to be an important factor at the two extremes of the economic scale. Those who are at the top of the social class continuum presumably suffer from stresses of work and important changes in their status, and those at the bottom, from poverty, hopelessness, and insecurity. During periods of great unemployment, like those that occurred from 1929 to 1933 and after World War II, marked increases in the *male* suicide rate have been observed, particularly in the age group from thirty-five to seventy-four, and strikingly in the group aged forty-five to fifty-four. Correlations with economic conditions and total unemployment rates are much lower for the suicide rates of women than of men. The change in social and occupational role and the psychologic trauma of unemployment appear to become especially stressful for men.

Variations in suicide rates by occupational groups are often conflicting and sometimes astonishing. Among some professional groups, however, striking differences have been reported from Great Britain and also the United States. Certain groups of professionals (physicians, dentists, lawyers) have been found to have the highest suicide rates registered, whereas others in the same social class (teachers, clergymen) have had low, even extremely low, rates.

Durkheim (78) believed that suicidal tendencies exist everywhere and that a moderate rate of suicide is normal and always present. When the rate increases and suicide becomes a problem it is not because of psychopathology or heredity or any other specific factors but rather a result of the failure of society as a whole, with all its dynamic forces, to fulfill the needs of each of its members. More contemporary concern with the psychology of suicide has brought to light many psychodynamic forces which supplement some of Durkheim's broad social views. While it is true, in Durkheim's sense, that a suicide is a suicide, whether it is the direct or indirect result of a positive or negative act, and that therefore a man who refuses to eat is as much a suicide as one who hangs himself, it adds to our understanding to consider that it is a very different thing to let oneself die than to kill oneself, as Bibring (23) has noted. Tabachnik and Farberow (330) have suggested that self-destructive tendencies are continuously distributed in the population and may vary quantitatively in an individual from time to time. They view self-destruction, a term they prefer because it is a specific psychologic construct, as a phenomenon of human existence. They have proposed a comprehensive check list of various intrapersonal and interpersonal characteristics that may serve as an indication of self-destructive potentiality, and may perhaps be applied to the general population.

Persons who perform suicidal acts have been classified into three groups. Almost one-third mean to solve their problem in a final way (the "intentioned" attempters that Shneidman and Farberow (307) have described); this group includes many more men than women. Another third is comprised of those who "cry for help" and are not serious in their effort to end their lives, the "contra-intentioned," the "manipulative suicides," the group in which women predominate. The third group is an intermediate, undecided one, the "sub-intentioned," who do not know how to solve their problems and may act on impulse. The majority of unsuccessful attempts, by both men and women, are made by young people under thirty-five years of age; the majority of those who succeed in committing suicide are older.

Clearly, there are many factors associated with suicide, if not causally related to it.

MENTAL ILLNESS AS A FACTOR IN SUICIDE

Many observers have been interested in estimating the contribution of mental illness to acts of self-destruction. Kraepelin (167) believed that at least one third of all suicides in Germany were caused by mental derangement. In the United States, Stearns (321) reported in 1921 that one half of the suicides he studied in Massachusetts had had recognized mental illness, and Cavan (46) estimated that 20 percent of the suicides in Chicago in 1923 could definitely be said to have been insane on the basis of information in the coroners' records. In an analysis of over 22,000 suicides among industrial policyholders of the Metropolitan Life Insurance Company in 1927, Dublin (73) found that 20 per cent had suffered from recognized mental disorder. Of suicide deaths with a secondary cause recorded in 1940 in the United States, mental disease and deficiency was the principal secondary cause, having been listed in about 39 per cent of these deaths (106).

Temoche, Pugh, and MacMahon (332) analyzed death certificates in Massachusetts for the three-year period 1949-51 and identified all deaths attributed to suicide. They were able to identify as psychiatrically ill only those persons who had been in mental institutions. They computed the following age-adjusted annual rates for the Massachusetts population:

Category of suicides	Number of suicides	Rate per 100,000 of specified category
Current mental hospital patients	30	17.6
Former mental hospital patients	147	47.7
Nonpatients	1,280	9.6

Rates for *current* male and female hospital patients were, respectively, 1.6 and 2.4 times higher than for the population without mental hospital experience, and for *former* male and female patients 3.7 and 8.5 times higher than the nonpatient rates. There was an increased risk for all diagnostic groups, but the most marked was for former mental hospital patients with depressive psychosis. (This is in accord with the frequent observation that suicidal risk is increased during the recovery phases of depression (42).)

In Dublin (Ireland) city and county, McCarthy and Walsh (221) studied coroners' records for the ten-year period 1954-63 and found that 32.7 per cent of the 315 suicides had previously been in psychiatric hospital and 6 per cent were in hospital at the time of the suicide (more than half of them in a psychiatric hospital). In Dublin, and by inference in Ireland, the suicide rate is said to be the lowest of all European rates; this is so even when the official rate of 2.2 is corrected by the investigators, for under-representation, to an average annual suicide rate twice that figure, 4.5 per 100,000 population.

In general, estimates of the contribution of mental illness to the suicide problem have varied widely but have hovered around 30-40 per cent. Contemporary estimates of mental disease as a factor in suicide tend to be higher than earlier ones.

Depressive Mental Illness as a Factor in Suicide

Depression preceding suicide is probably universal and may be a feature of all types of mental disease associated with suicide and, in fact, of all types of suicide. Depressive mental illness, while far from universal, has also been described as the most frequent type of mental disorder associated with self-destruction. Various subtypes of depressive disease have been held more or less responsible for suicide, but the essential characteristic has been pathologic depression.

Kraepelin linked suicide with melancholia, but not with the depressive stage of manic-depressive insanity in which depression and elation alternate. Others have also laid stress on the particular danger of suicidal tendencies in melancholia because action is not interfered with by retardation in the way it is in manic-depressive psychosis. Stenstedt, on the other hand, found the frequency of suicide among manic-depressives (325) higher than among involutional melancholiacs (326), although both exceeded the rates expected in the Swedish general population. Merrell (225) went so far as to suggest that suicide is an alternative expression of the genotype for manic-depressive tendency.

Sainsbury (292) summarized studies published up to about 1950 which offered findings about the relation of depressive mental disease to suicide. Of the half-dozen clinical studies listed, only that of Lendrum in Detroit (189) failed to show a strong association between depressive illness and suicide; Lendrum was evidently averse to making the diagnosis without a definite cyclic history. The other investigators found that, among suicides with mental disorder, from 20 to 44 per cent had been suffering from depressive psychoses.

In Figure 2 and Table 6, four studies published since 1955 which offer information on the role of depressive illness in suicide in the context of various population groups are presented. Three of them, by Sainsbury (292), Robins *et al.* (281), and Seager and Flood (302), are based on a careful review of information obtained from coroners' records and inquest proceedings, plus, in the case of the Robins study, supplementary information from interviews with key persons shortly after each suicide, and in the Seager and Flood study, an examination of hospital and clinical records. The fourth study, that of Helgason (130), is part of the larger investigation of the epidemiology of mental disorders in Iceland.

The findings indicate a progressive increase over a period of time and with more intense investigation, both in the proportion of suicides with mental disorder and, of these, the proportion with depressive illness, as estimated by these investigators. The percentage of suicides with mental disorder ranged from 47 to 90; the percentage of depressive illness in all those with mental

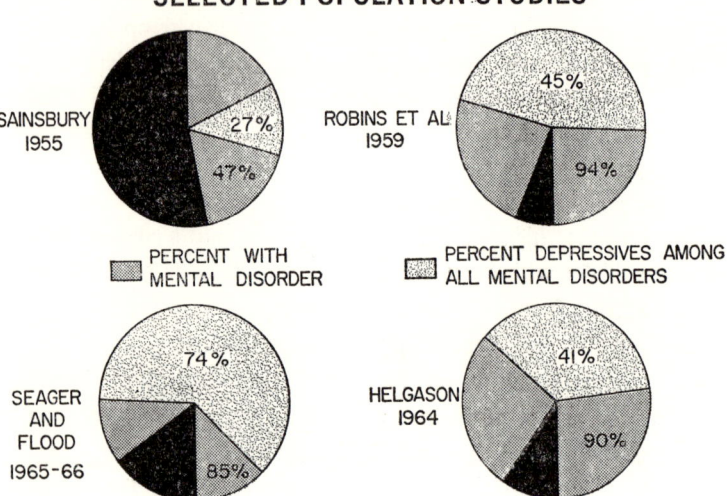

FIGURE 2.

DEPRESSIVE DISORDERS AMONG SUICIDES WITH MENTAL DISORDERS SELECTED POPULATION STUDIES

disorder ranged from 27 to 74. Regardless of the differences in proportions, there was no diagnostic category which approached the order of magnitude of the contribution of depressive illness to suicide. Attention was drawn to alcoholism as the second most frequent diagnosis in the study of Robins and colleagues.

Seager and Flood diagnosed their group of depressives as 18 per cent neurotic and 55 per cent endogenous. Robins and co-workers do not accept the separate diagnosis of neurotic de-

Table 6. DEPRESSIVE DISORDERS AMONG SUICIDES WITH MENTAL DISORDERS. SELECTED POPULATION STUDIES

Authors	Year of Publication	Source of Data	No. of Suicides	Those with Mental Disorder (%)	Depressives Among All Mental Disorders (%)	Suicide Rate per 100,000 General Population
Sainsbury	1955	N. London, 5 boroughs, coroners' records, 3 yrs., 1936–38	390	47	27	14.1
Robins et al.	1959	St. Louis, Missouri, coroners' records and interviews shortly after suicides, 1 year, 1956–57	134	94	45	11.7[a]
Seager and Flood	1965	Bristol, England, coroners' records and hospital and clinic records, 5 years, 1957–61	325	85	74	8.0
Helgason	1964	Iceland, cohort born 1895–97 and alive in 1910 (5,395); by 1957, 1,498 deaths	51	90	41	

[a] 1960 rate.

pression and considered all their cases to be manic-depressive, involutional, or depressive psychoses. Helgason diagnosed only 6 per cent (one case) as neurotic depression; the others were classed as manic-depressive psychosis.

The probability of suicide in a patient with a psychotic depressive illness is much greater after the age of forty, Robins *et al.* reported from St. Louis. In London, Sainsbury found that 55 per cent of the middle-aged and elderly were described as depressed at the time of their suicide, as compared with only 40 per cent of the younger cases; the numbers with clinically recognizable depressive illness, however, were about two-thirds of these figures. In a study of suicide in later life which stressed the important role of social factors (293), he noted that depressive illness is a more widely recognized precursor of suicide than is organic mental disorder.

Sainsbury has also made comparisons between suicide and hospital depression rates. Finding social class differences between suicides and depressives, he then compared age-sex specific rates for first admissions to mental hospital for depression with similar rates for suicides in the general population (Appendix Table 7) and concluded that suicides and depressives over the age of forty-five years were two distinct populations.

Studies of the nature and extent of association between depression and suicide are not likely to be furthered by comparisons of such rates. Suicide rates reflect adjudged suicides in the total population from all causes (of which depression presumably is one); hospital depression rates reflect only part of the treated segment of the entire depressive population (which may be largely untreated or unreported). As Reid (275) has noted, reactive depressions frequently underlie suicides, but cause no rise in the hospital admission rate.

SUICIDE IN DEPRESSIVE MENTAL ILLNESS

Data prepared by Horatio Pollock on the diagnoses of 200 suicides in the mental hospitals of New York State between 1919 and 1929 (72) showed that the highest suicide rates occurred in the group of patients with involutional melancholia, and the next highest in those with manic-depressive psychosis. The only other conditions importantly related to suicide, but very far below the depressive conditions, were general paresis, alcoholism, and schizophrenia, in that order. Suicide mortality was highest for both men and women with involutional melancholia and manic-depressive psychosis, but it was much higher

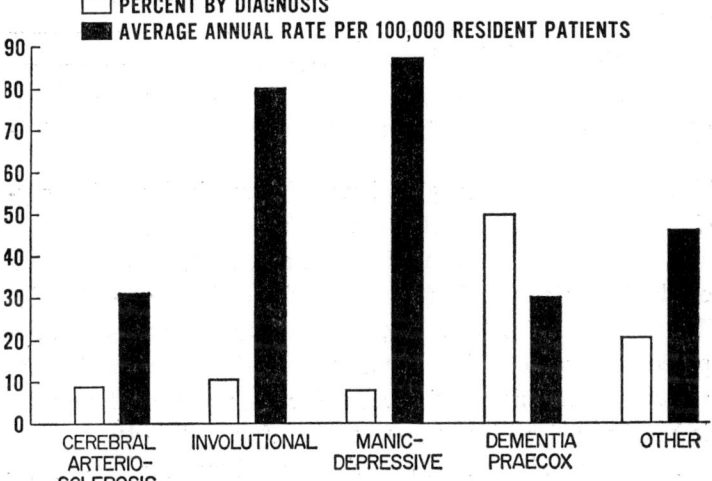

FIGURE 3.

SUICIDES AMONG PATIENTS WITH MENTAL DISEASE IN NEW YORK CIVIL STATE HOSPITALS APRIL, 1957-MARCH, 1959

among male than female patients. The male suicide rate was, in fact, higher than the female rate in all forms of mental disease.

Figure 3 and Table 7 are based on unpublished material prepared by Malzberg and presented by Dublin. Suicides among patients with mental disease in New York State hospitals are presented for the two-year period from April, 1957 to March, 1959, by type of mental disorder and average annual rate of suicide per 100,000 resident patients with the specified disorder.

Table 7. SUICIDES AMONG PATIENTS WITH MENTAL DISEASE IN NEW YORK CIVIL STATE HOSPITALS, APRIL, 1957–MARCH, 1959[a]

Mental Disorder	Suicides Number	Suicides Per cent	Average Annual Rate per 100,000 Resident Patients*
Total	62	100	34.0
Alcoholic	—	—	—
With cerebral arteriosclerosis	6	9.7	31.9
Senile	—	—	—
Involutional	7	11.3	80.4
Manic-depressive	5	8.1	87.4
Dementia praecox	31	50.0	30.1
Other	13	21.0	46.1

* With specified disorder. Resident March 31, 1958.

[a] This table has been taken verbatim from: Dublin, L. I.: *Suicide: A Sociological and Statistical Study*. New York: The Ronald Press Company, 1963. It is based on personal correspondence with Dr. Benjamin Malzberg.

The suicide *rates* among patients with manic-depressive psychosis (87.4) and involutional melancholia (80.4) are far above the next two diagnostic categories, mental disorder with cerebral arteriosclerosis (31.9) and dementia praecox (30.1). The problem of suicide is greater, of course, among schizophrenics, because their number in hospitals is so great, but the association of suicide with a specific type of mental disorder in hospital patients is strongest for the affective disorder.

In Monroe County, New York State, where there is a cumulative psychiatric case register to which all psychiatric experiences for county residents have been routinely reported since 1960, Gardner and co-workers (99) found a similar association. They also noted that suicide rates for neurotic or personality disorders, as well as for affective psychoses, were more than twice as high after fifty-five than before that age. This age differential for the diagnosis of neurotic or personality disorders suggested to them that depressive symptomatology is often missed in the elderly, among whom depression is far more common than is recognized and in whom it is a precursor to suicide.

Robins and colleagues summarized five large follow-up studies of death by suicide in manic-depressive disease, reported in the European literature between 1938 and 1952, and concluded that approximately 14 per cent of manic-depressives will take their own lives in one or another episode of the disease. This is not a supportable assumption on the basis of the data presented (Appendix Table 8), since proportionate mortality has been equated with case fatality. The five follow-up studies, reported at different times from different areas for vastly different periods of observation, showed deaths by suicide in persons of unspecified age and sex with manic-depressive psychosis to range from 3.3 to 14.3 per cent. As it happened, the percentages of deaths from all causes which were attributable to suicide came out to roughly 14 per cent in four of the five studies. Further work is needed to find out what proportion of depressives commit suicide and to determine their clinical and epidemiologic characteristics.

Attempted Suicide, Mental Illness, and Depressive Mental Illness

Durkheim (78) claimed that whereas suicide and attempted suicide were often discussed as if they were separate phenomena, actual suicides must be regarded as those attempts which succeed. On clinical grounds, Stengel and Cook in England (322) have sought to demonstrate that attempted suicide is a different problem from suicide itself, often a form of appeal, and Farberow and Shneidman in Los Angeles (90) have delineated many of the characteristics of those who attempt suicide.

The frequency of attempted suicide decreases with advancing age, whereas the incidence of suicide increases; males predominate in successful suicides, whereas many more females attempt suicide. The frequency of depressive illness is less in attempted suicide than in successful suicide (293). The two groups overlap, however, and they do so to a greater extent among the elderly, whose attempts are often of a serious kind. Batchelor and Napier (17) found 47 per cent of suicide attempts in those aged sixty and over to be related to a depressive illness; O'Neal et al. (250) found 70 per cent of attempts in the elderly to be associated with severe depression.

Ettlinger and Flordh (88) studied 500 consecutive cases of attempted suicide at a large municipal hospital in Stockholm, during a fifteen-month period in 1952-53. Diagnoses of depressive conditions were involutional melancholia, 2.2 per cent; other endogenous depressive states, 4.6 per cent; and neurotic depression, 24 per cent. In the total series, females predominated, as they did in the depressive categories. Among the seventeen attempts which resulted in death, however, there were more males than females, even though reactive depression was the most frequent diagnosis.

A study by Stengel (324) covering a follow-up period of up to eighteen years showed that many who attempt suicide try again, and that about 10 per cent finally succeed. A similar study by Ringel, covering a shorter period, shows a correspondingly lower proportion of 5 per cent who eventually become suicides. Attempted suicides are said to be about eight to ten times more frequent than actual suicides.

The numerous observations of a strong association between depressive mental illness and suicide, related to both the contribution of depression to suicide and the termination of depression in suicide, warrant consideration of suicide as the mortality of depressive mental illness.

IV

SOME CHARACTERISTICS OF PERSONS WITH DEPRESSION

Sex

There appear to be no exceptions to the generalization that depression is more common in women than in men, whether it is the feeling of depression, neurotic depression, or depressive psychosis. Not only in morbidity surveys of depression, however, is this an invariable finding. In general health surveys such as the United States National Health Survey and the British Survey of Sickness, more illness or incapacity is found in women than in men, regardless of the case definition of illness or disability, precision of study methods, socioeconomic status, or place of residence (211).

With regard to mortality, however, the picture is reversed. Mortality in depression, as measured by suicide, is greater in males than in females, as it is for suicides from all causes. And mortality for the majority of other chronic conditions to which both men and women are heir is higher for men. The frequent relationship of high morbidity with low mortality in women, and low morbidity with high mortality in men, has been noted in other fields of health (70). MacMahon *et al.* (211) speculate that either females admit to illness more readily or that they experience a higher incidence of illness which is less lethal. They note further that at times the disparity between male and female death rates has been observed to be greatest during the age period between fifteen and thirty-nine years, the childbearing years of females (except where standards of obstetric care are poor).

Many attempts have been made to associate depression, and other emotional or psychiatric disorder, with female endocrine-physiologic processes. Psychologic changes with the menstrual cycle have been widely described, and mild depression, restlessness, or tension a few days before the period is commonplace. A "menstrual psychosis" has not materialized when careful and honest diaries have been kept (193). Some findings suggest that endocrine physiology may influence the *timing* of certain psychiatric events, such as the suicidal act in women (209), admission to hospital for attempted suicide (63, 337), and entrance to hospital for acute psychiatric illnesses, including depression (63).

Efforts to associate hysterectomy with mental disorder have not been successful. In several unpublished studies (238) it was found that women who have had hysterectomies by age forty do not appear to have higher rates of mental illness than

SEX

other women; women studied before and after hysterectomy showed no change in frequency of mental illness; and, when a difference was found between women who had and who had not had hysterectomies, it was also found that more hysterectomized women had had a prior history of mental disorder. Bragg (32) reported less depressive illness in women who had had a hysterectomy than those who had undergone cholecystectomy, as judged by mental hospital admissions.

The effect of childbearing on mental disorder has long been a subject of interest and inquiry. The prevailing view, that mental illness associated with childbearing is no different from that unrelated to childbirth (336), seems uncontested clinically for the pregnancy phase of childbearing; that is to say, pregnancy is not implicated in the development of prepartum mental illness. As far as mental disturbances which occur after delivery are concerned, however, there is a general air of dissatisfaction with this view and investigations continue to be carried out about frequency of occurrence, clinical features, and probable etiology of postpartum mental illness (122). Several epidemiologic studies have reopened these and related issues and have drawn attention to the problem of depression.

Pugh and co-workers (266) studied the relation of childbearing to mental illness by determining the observed and expected numbers of first admissions to public and private mental hospitals among the childbearing population of Massachusetts women who were, or had ever been, married (aged fifteen to forty-four) in 1950. During the entire period of *pregnancy,* there were significantly *fewer* admissions than expected, in all categories of psychiatric diagnosis (psychoses, psychoneuroses, and personality disturbances). During the nine-month *postpartum* observation period, there was a significantly *greater* number of admissions with psychosis, most marked during the first three months after delivery, when a smaller excess was also noted for nonpsychotic admissions. The manic-depressive group made up 53 per cent of the total excess in psychoses and was the only specific psychotic group for which the excess was statistically significant.

From their data they were unable to determine whether the deficit of hospital admissions for psychosis during pregnancy could most adequately be explained by a delay in admission until after delivery (compatible with their findings), a lower average risk of pregnancy among the patients than the general population (a possibility), or an actual protective effect of pregnancy against the occurrance of psychosis (not determinable).

For the first three months of the *postpartum* period, they estimated an annual *added risk,* from causes operating during that period, of 1.8-2.5 first admissions with psychosis per 1,000 married women in that stage of the puerperium. The additional risk was estimated to be considerably higher for the first six weeks after delivery, namely 3.0-3.6 per 1,000.

Other studies of mental illness in parous women of childbearing age who were or had been married were made in Cincinnati and Hamilton County, Ohio, by Paffenbarger (252, 253) and Paffenbarger and McCabe (255), also using psychiatric hospital admissions as the index of mental disease. Study subjects were chosen from the obstetric records of the Cincinnati hospitals; they were the patients who were pregnant or had been delivered up to six months before the time of onset of first psychosis. Control subjects were the obstetric patients who were delivered just before and just after the study patients, matched only by race.

It was also found in this study that there was a low incidence of mental illness during pregnancy (interpreted as suggesting a protective effect of pregnancy), but an added risk during the postpartum period was not observed; the rates for the first six postpartum months approximated those for a comparable nonchildbearing group. The investigators drew attention, however, to the striking characteristics of postpartum mental illness, such as its explosive peak following the lull of the prepartum period, and its abrupt impact, and believed that these were most probably related to endocrine-somatic etiologic factors, rather than to psychic disturbances. They noted that when mental illness recurred in subsequent pregnancies, it was consistently replicated as either prepartum or postpartum (255). Depression was a frequent symptom in postpartum illness.

In the initial phase of these studies it was found that during the eighteen-year period 1940-58, a total of 126 pregnant patients (ninety-six white and thirty Negro) had experienced their first recognized psychotic attack. Of the 126, there were 45 per cent diagnosed as having schizophrenia, 21 per cent with manic-depressive psychosis, and 33 per cent undifferentiated by clinical type (252). All were subsequently considered as a composite group because no differences related to prenatal or perinatal factors were found among the diagnostic types.

More detailed analysis for the last two-year period, 1957-58, revealed that of a total of fifty cases of postpartum psychoses, thirty-two were first attacks, six were recurrences in women who had experienced a previous postpartum episode, and twelve were reactivations in women whose prior attacks had been unassociated with pregnancy. The incidence of postpartum psychoses of all diagnostic categories, among white women, was 0.6 for first attacks and 1.0 for total illnesses per 1,000 live births. Among Negro women, comparable rates were 1.3 for first attacks and 1.9 for all psychoses per 1,000 live births.

For some of the analyses, the study population was extended to include those developing psychoneuroses as well as psychoses, and the data for both groups were pooled for analysis "since the two groups were similar as regards most of the obstetric factors that proved to be associated with the development of a parapartum illness" (253). For the same reason it was believed that findings for first attacks could be pooled with those for previous attacks unassociated with childbearing, and that white and Negro subjects could be combined.

The shifting study criteria and study groups, the combinations of subgroups (to add stability to the small numbers involved) on the basis of lack of disparity in obstetric variables, and the relative inattention to the specifics of psychopathology detract from the conclusiveness of some of the findings.

Age

For depressions, as for most disorders, variations with age are greater than they are with other variables. Because association with age is a highly important characteristic, Ödegaard at one time suggested that a way to overcome the discouraging task of comparing statistical data from various geographic areas with different schools of psychiatric thought was to disregard diagnosis altogether and simply use age distribution. The generalization can be made at this time that depression is reported to be rare in infancy and childhood, makes its clinical appearance in adolescence, increases in young adulthood, reaches its greatest frequency in the middle years, and may decline somewhat in the later years of life.

Anaclitic depression is a term first used by Spitz (317) to describe affective disturbance in infants and to indicate its psychodynamic roots. Studies on the psychiatric effects of "hospitalism" (318) led to the designation of a depressive syndrome in infants under one year of age who suffered severe disturbance during an unbroken three-month period of absence of their mothers, during the sixth through eighth months of their life. These infants have been described by others as institutional psychopaths (22).

Depression is rarely diagnosed before the age of puberty. Suicides (over 100 a year are reported in the United States among children less than fifteen years old), and attempted suicides, are generally not attributed to depressive disorder (349). Lourie studied children aged three to fourteen years who attempted suicide and found there were no depressions in the usual clinical sense, only situational depressions (205). In recent years, increasing attention has been directed to depression in adolescents and young adults because of the rising problem of suicide (67).

It is probably fair to say that the factor of age has often influenced the diagnosis of psychotic affective disorders and, thereby, also the reported age distribution of these illnesses. Schizophrenia (dementia praecox) has been thought of as a disorder of younger people; depression as an ailment of middle-aged and older persons. The age differences in hospitalized patients are illustrated by a comparison of median ages of first admissions and resident patients in public mental hospitals in the United States in 1957 (7).

	Median Age in Years	
Psychotic Disorders	First Admissions	Resident Patients
Involutional psychotic reaction	54.3	62.2
Manic-depressive reaction	45.2	61.3
Schizophrenic reaction	33.7	50.0

Rates of admission to the Maryland psychiatric case register, per 1,000 population, for fiscal year 1963 (239) reached their peak for both manic-depressive and involutional depressive reactions in the age group between forty-five and sixty-four (0.18 and 0.06, respectively); and for psychotic depressive reaction, in the group sixty-five years and over (0.20). The pattern for psychoneurotic depressive reaction, however, was quite different. A marked peak was reached in the age group between twenty-five and forty-four (1.07) and an almost equal rate was recorded for those aged from forty-five to sixty-four years (0.99). The peak for all affective disorders, psychotic and neurotic, was seen in the age group from forty-five to sixty-four (1.41). On Martha's Vineyard, during 1962-66, Mazer (219) found the highest rate for all reported depressive disorders to be in the age group from twenty-five to thirty-four, which was entirely the result of an unusual excess of women.

Involutional melancholia is the prototype for disorders of the involutional age (these may be of the depressive, paranoid, or mixed types). In its classical form it is an anxious, agitated, delusional depression of the menopause. It affects women from the fourth decade on, and men beginning in the fifth decade, in a ratio of about three to one, according to Bigelow (24). Gregory states that the diagnosis has increased somewhat in popularity during recent years, particularly in males, and is largely restricted to the forty- to seventy-year age range (114). There has been nothing but disagreement about the separation of this group from the manic-depressive psychoses, a legacy of Kraepelin's classification. Neither clinically nor epidemiologically is there any justification for this, according to Ödegaard and Gruenberg; Beck (18) reports no evidence for agitation as a distinguishing characteristic; and Szalita (329) finds no psychoanalytic basis for differentiation. Kallmann (153), on the other hand, believes involutional melancholia is not connected with manic-depressive psychosis, either clinically or genetically. (In the Eighth Revision of the International Classification of Diseases, involutional melancholia is listed with manic-depressive psychosis.)

ETHNIC GROUP

There is a vast literature on mental disorder in peoples of various cultures, according to race, nativity, religion, and other characteristics. Observations range from the complete absence of mental disorder (as in the Anabaptist sect of Hutterites when Eaton and Weil undertook their study) to the designation of a national affliction (the "English Malady" of suicide described by Cheyne in the eighteenth century). The observations are largely impressionistic and often misleading because of great differences in form and content of mental disturbance and societal attitudes towards it, not only among cultures, but also in the same cultures at different periods of time. It has been said (3) that a normal person of the Middle Ages might easily be thought to be abnormal today. From an epidemiologic point of view, all these difficulties are compounded by the usual failure to relate mental disturbance to the population at risk.

Cross-cultural studies of the depressive disorders have been reviewed by Stainbrook (320), Kardiner (155), Wittkower and Rin (351), Montagu (230), and others. Murphy and colleagues (237) recently reported on a questionnaire survey of psychiatrists in many parts of the world regarding their views of the frequency of a basic depressive disorder (a mood of depression, diurnal mood changes, insomnia with early morning wakening, and diminution of interest in social environment) and of other symptoms such as thought retardation, guilt, and self-depreciation. The methodologic shortcomings of the survey are insuperable; they make it impossible to accept the authors' preliminary conclusions that the frequency of psychotic depression in a community does not appear to be related to the specific culture, to the nature or intensity of religious beliefs held, or to social class or residence, but rather to the level of cohesion in the community; and that the association between guilt feelings and depression is independent of the frequency of depression as defined, and independent of the association between depression and suicidal ideas, but is strongly related to the Christian or Judeo-Christian tradition.

Caudill and Doi (45) refer to "the air of mild depression that pervades Japanese life" and the high suicide rate, particularly of persons between the ages of fifteen and twenty-four. Katchadourian (157) has studied the prevalence of mental illness among the Christians and Moslems of Lebanon and reported more depressive psychosis among the Christians, but about equal frequencies of mania in the two groups. Manic-depressive reactions were found to be relatively rare in a community of recent immigrants to Israel (216).

Quite consistently, until the 1950's, depression was reported as being rare or nonexistent in Africa (and in some other primitive cultures). More recently, some of the symptoms of depression and some instances of classical forms have been described. In a study of mental disorder among the Yoruba of Western Nigeria, Leighton and colleagues (182) were able to elicit many of the symptoms of the depressive syndrome, although the concept of depression was not known there. The only items missing that are commonly seen in European and American cases were guilt and self-reproach. Such symptoms did not appear often in the Nova Scotia survey sample either, but according to the investigators, this may have been due to failure to try to elicit them. In Ghana, West Africa, relatively high proportions of hospitalized manic-depressives, depressives, nonhospitalized depressives, and attempted suicides have been reported (345). In Ethiopia as well, depressive states are reported to be common and to be associated with feelings of guilt (but manic phases are rare); suicides and attempted suicides are not infrequent (338).

Differing reports of low prevalence of depression among Africans led Asuni (10) to investigate suicide as an index of depression. He found a very low suicide rate in Western Nigeria, the lowest one reported anywhere in the world (under one per 100,000), and concluded that depression was probably rare *if* depressive illness did not manifest itself in that country by feelings of guilt, unworthiness, and self-reproach, with the consequent tendency to self-destruction. Rao (270) likewise attempted to use suicide as an index of depression in southern

India. He concluded there was no direct relationship between suicide and depression in that area because depression occurred infrequently, with different symptomatology from that seen in western countries, and the suicide rate (43/100,000) was high. He observed that only 4 per cent of psychiatric admissions to one hospital during a three-year period were diagnosed as cases of depression and doubted that Easterners are susceptible to depression. Carstairs (43) noted that private practitioners in India say that they do not find depression rare.

Migration

An appraisal of studies of the relationship between migration and mental illness was recently made by Murphy (236). Ödegaard's early work on emigration and mental disease among the Norwegian-born in Minnesota (243), using first hospital admission as an index, is a classic in the field. While schizophrenia, general paresis, and alcoholic psychosis all occurred more frequently in the immigrants (Norwegian-born in Minnesota) than among the natives (Norwegians of Norway), only the affective psychoses showed a reverse distribution, being slightly more frequent among the natives than among the immigrants. Ödegaard favored and has continued to favor the self-selection hypothesis over the environmental one in explaining the differentials in rates of endogenous psychoses between immigrants and natives. He believes that psychologic-constitutional factors, more than the hardships of immigrant life, account for both the excess emigration of schizoid types and the lack of tendency for syntonic (depressive) types to leave home. The data for schizophrenia, in the opinion of Kohn (166), can be interpreted equally validly by social selection or social causation.

In early studies of mental disease in New York State according to nativity and parentage, Malzberg (212) found higher frequencies among the foreign-born, but did not find depression to be an exception (Ödegaard's comparison of his findings with those of Malzberg is reproduced as Appendix Table 9). Later on, Malzberg (215) again showed the rates for foreign-born in 1939-41 to be higher than those for natives with affective psychoses, but only for females. Malzberg has consistently interpreted his data, which are essentially similar to those of Ödegaard in most respects, as a reflection of the stresses of migration and resettlement. The nativity status of treated depressives has also been studied by others in New York (262), New Haven (280), and Texas (144), with generally similar interpretations.

More recent studies of migration have focused on internal instead of external migration. Migrants within a country reflect a different type of selection processes and face much less environmental stress than overseas immigrants. Ödegaard has since contradicted his earlier findings and reports significantly lower hospital admission rates among migrants than among nonmigrants, especially for schizophrenia (9). He infers from this that the type and direction of the migration is decisive. Migrants from cities tend to have higher rates, probably because this type of migration is more atypical of the population. The city of Oslo, however, was found to be an exception in that migrants to the city had higher rates than the city-born, particularly women (62). In Helsinki, it is reported (156) that the incidence of mental disorders is lower among recent migrants into the city than among the rest of the population, with the most marked differences in the group of manic-depressives and involutional psychoses.

Race

In the United States, studies of depressive disorders among Negroes have been reported by a number of investigators. Faris and Dunham (91) found no striking racial differences except

ETHNIC GROUP

for the low percentage of Negroes with the depressed type of manic-depressive psychosis in Chicago in 1922-34. Wagner (342) reported fewer new admissions of Negroes to the psychiatric pavilion of the Cincinnati General Hospital during 1936-37 for involutional psychosis, but higher rates for Negroes than for whites for manic-depressive psychosis. Malzberg and Lee (215) reported lower rates for Negro first admissions than for whites, for manic-depressive psychosis, at the New York State mental hospitals during 1939-41. Frumkin (97) found hospital admissions in Ohio in 1952 for involutional psychosis to be lower for Negro males and females than for whites. Duval *et al.* (79) found first admissions for all types of psychoneuroses higher for nonwhites than for whites, in a sample study covering almost all mental hospitals, psychiatric clinics, and psychiatric units in general hospitals in Ohio during the period from July 1, 1958 to December 31, 1961. And Simon (308) found involutional psychosis lower in Negro women than in white women, when first admissions to the Jackson Memorial psychiatric hospital in Miami were compared for the five-year period 1959-63.

In Maryland, in the 1963 fiscal year, reports to the central psychiatric register from all mental hospitals, psychiatric clinics, and psychiatric services in general hospitals showed the rates for all mental disorders *except* the affective disorders to be higher among Negro males and females than among white groups (239). This held for each type of affective reaction except involutional reaction, which was a little higher for Negro females than for white females. Almost three decades earlier, in Baltimore, a morbidity survey revealed a disproportionately small percentage of Negroes with psychoneurosis, including reactive depression (187).

McGough and co-workers (222) recently described the changing patterns of psychiatric illness among Negroes in the southern United States and noted the effect of racial integration of a psychiatric hospital on the diagnostic categories of Negro patients admitted, compared with white patients and Negro patients at a segregated hospital. Among the new population of fifty-five Negro patients admitted to a previously all-white hospital during the first year of integration, 1963-64, there was a significantly higher proportion of psychotic depression than in either the white or Negro control populations. Psychoneurotic depression was found to be slightly less frequent than in the white population but much more common than in the all-Negro hospital. The authors predict a rise in the reported frequency of depressive conditions and in hospital admissions, as treatment facilities become more available for the southern Negro.

Social Class and Related Characteristics

The vast literature on social, economic, and environmental variables in mental disturbance deals for the most part with mental disorders as a group or as psychoses or neuroses. A notable exception is the diagnostic category of schizophrenia, to which much attention has been given because, as has been said (166), the epidemiologic findings for severe mental illness seem to parallel those for schizophrenia. Depressive conditions are infrequently specified.

The great contribution of Faris and Dunham (91) to our understanding of the social epidemiology of mental disorder has been followed by too few studies that go beyond the original observations. The essential findings of the 1922-34 Chicago study with respect to manic-depressive psychosis (which was found to be unlike schizophrenia in almost every respect) were as follows: (1) the pattern of cases was a random one; neither high nor low rates were distributed in any systematic fashion throughout the city; (2) the same typical random distribution held for male and female manic-depressives; (3) the same random pattern was seen in the distribution of rates for private and state hospitals, both for local communities and subcommunities; (4) the rates for the separate types, manic and depressed, were also random in their distribution; (5) approximately the same number of communities had high rates as had low rates; (6) the percentages of cases in each quartile were approximately the same for the manic and the depressed types, indicating an absence of any definite concentration of cases; and (7) the rates according to nativity and race by housing areas show the same lack of pattern.

In addition to these characteristics there were others which were also in marked contrast to the findings for schizophrenia. There were larger numbers of married than of single persons of *both* sexes among the manic and depressed types (only married *women* predominated among schizophrenics); there were no striking racial differences in the manic-depressive rates, except for the low percentage of Negroes in the depressed type; there was a tendency, although it was not clearly defined, for the manic-depressive cases to come from urban areas with a fairly high economic, housing, and cultural level; 50 per cent of the manic-depressive cases were admitted to private hospitals; there was a preponderance of females over males in the total manic-depressive group and for each age group under thirty-nine years; after age fifty, however, the male rate was higher for every age period except fifty to fifty-four.

A distribution was made of all cases diagnosed as psychoneurosis at both private and state hospitals; although the numbers were small, the pattern seemed somewhat similar to that for manic-depressive psychosis. Lemkau *et al.* (187) remarked on the female preponderance in both adult neurotics and manic-depressive psychotics in the Baltimore survey of 1936, a relationship not seen with any other psychosis, which suggested certain basic similarities between the two groups.

Other studies of diagnosed cases, using first hospital admissions as in the Chicago study, or admissions to a broader range of psychiatric treatment services, have generally reported similar or related findings: a greater scatter of manic-depressive cases than of schizophrenics in five other American cities (in one of which it was said that no correlation exists between manic-depressive psychosis and schizophrenia) (300); a lack of relationship between depressive disorders and social factors, in contrast to the significant relationship between schizophrenia and social variables such as socioeconomic status, ethnicity, and community and family stability (29); the more frequent diagnosis of affective psychoses among people in comfortable circumstances and better occupations than among the poor and unskilled, in contrast to schizophrenia (126, 163, 335); the greater use of private hospitals by those with affective psychoses than by schizophrenics, and the similarities between depressive psychosis and psychoneurotic or personality disorder with respect to follow-up experience after hospital discharge (100).

Some investigators, on the other hand, have reported an inverse relationship with social class, or a failure to establish a lack of relationship. Hollingshead and Redlich (136), for example, found that first admissions to treatment for psychoses of all types, and for depressive neuroses, in New Haven, were inversely related to social class, although the least variation was observed for the affective disorders. Ödegaard (247) has been unable to confirm the greater frequency of hospitalized manic-depressive psychosis in higher social classes in Norway, but notes that the differential among classes is much less marked for the affective psychoses than for schizophrenia. Similar findings made by Brooke in England and Wales are shown in Appendix Table 10. The midtown Manhattan symptom prevalence study in the general population (175) reported a consistent inverse correlation

SOCIAL CLASS

between symptom patterns, including depression, and socioeconomic status.

Marital Status

For the functional psychoses *as a whole,* excessively high rates of admission to mental hospitals of single and divorced persons, as compared with the married group, have been repeatedly observed in the United States (172, 267), Britain (33, 242), Norway (244, 246), and other countries; they are illustrated in Appendix Figure 3. This strong association between admission rates and marital status is not observed for manic-depressive psychosis; the extent to which manic-depressive psychosis differs from this pattern is illustrated in the findings of Faris and Dunham shown in Appendix Table 11.

In other studies the differences are either not as marked (212), or persons with psychotic depression are found as likely to be married as single, and only somewhat more likely to be divorced (244, 301), or "only for manic-depressive psychosis is the female excess independent of marital status" (248). Widowhood is reported to confer only a small increased risk of hospital admission; immediate depressive reactions to bereavement, among women, are thought to contribute to the modest rate increase (246).

Marriage and fertility rates of manic-depressive patients have been investigated in the course of other investigations. Kallmann (153) reported on marriage and fertility rates of manic-depressive patients in his twin studies, finding that psychotic subjects married less frequently, tended more often to remain childless when married, and produced fewer children if fertile, as compared with their nonpsychotic twin partners and siblings, or normal controls. Ödegaard (247) studied the marital state of Norwegian patients before their first hospital admission and also reported a lower marriage rate, a somewhat lower marital fertility rate, and a decreased reproduction rate compared to the general population. Essen-Möller (85) found the marriage rate of Swedish manic-depressives to be normal before their illness and decreased by about half after illness, but with no differences from the general population in fertility or reproductive rate in either period. Lewis (194) obtained similar results in England but cautioned that the situation may change rapidly with new treatment methods and changed patterns of hospitalization. Nothing is known of the relative contribution of involuntary and voluntary influences on fertility.

Urban-rural comparisons of admissions to mental hospitals have quite consistently shown more admissions from urban areas. Malzberg (212) found these variations in New York State to be independent of age differences in the communities of varying size, but related to factors of sex and diagnostic category. The standardized rate of first admissions with manic-depressive psychoses was higher in the urban population in the ratio of 1.3 to 1 (for dementia praecox the ratio was 1.8 to 1). The rates did not vary directly with population; however, as was the case with dementia praecox, there was a tendency for female rates to be higher and male rates lower from the larger cities. Clausen and Kohn (49) found no differences in admission rates for manic-depressive psychosis between a small city and the surrounding county but, as seen in Table 2, the situation was markedly changed to resemble the urban-rural pattern when services were provided close by and attitudes toward hospitalization became more favorable. Increased hospitalization for depressions has been reported in rapidly growing suburban areas (344).

Occupation

Among hospitalized patients, manic-depressive psychosis has

been variously described as inversely related to occupational status (212); nearly equally distributed (for single women) among the various occupational groups (248); more closely associated with the type of activity than with the social level within each trade (247); and not correlated in any way with high income and high prestige, in contrast to all other psychoses (47). The frequent observation that manic-depressive psychosis is more common in the higher social and occupational classes cannot be confirmed, but most studies show an absence of the inverse relationship to social class that is uniformly reported for schizophrenia.

General

The problem of distortion of findings based on hospitalized populations has been reviewed by Cooper (58) from the vantage point of both hospital and general practice statistics available for mental disorders in Great Britain. The variance is indicated by the failure to find, in general practice, an excess of single persons comparable with the preponderance shown by mental hospital statistics, or the excess of persons from the lowest social class, or any urban-rural differences for psychoses.

Hammer and Leacock (125) assembled and analyzed data from epidemiologic studies, up to 1959, in which social class, ethnic, rural-urban, and geographic mobility correlates of mental illness were investigated. Although the lack of comparability of most of the studies and the inconclusiveness of their findings were all too clear, certain parallel trends within a number of the studies were evident: notably, the consistently different epidemiologic pattern of manic-depressive psychosis as compared with schizophrenia.

The marked differences in social experiences between those who subsequently develop affective psychoses and those who become schizophrenic, added to the unsatisfactory clinical foundations for the classification of mental disorders, have led Cassel (44) to suggest that a sociologic basis for classification might potentially be more useful for research. Schizophrenia is thus seen to have more in common with tuberculosis and suicide than with manic-depressive psychosis.

Clausen (48) urges more systematic work at the classification of individuals, not merely in relation to symptoms or the usual social variables but also in terms of more meaningful social experiences and interactions, such as the dominant features of one's life history, value orientations, social and cognitive skills, modes of coping and defense, and the character of social relationships, both intimate and secondary. The characteristics of a social class milieu, and particularly of the beliefs and practices of those who are members of it, give rise to particular personality patterns which affect socialization skills and deviance.

SEASONAL VARIATION

Climatic changes have been associated with the onset, course, and termination of the illness, but they appear to be nonspecific in their effects, so far as can be determined. Seasonal peaks, however, have been widely described for depressive illness. Spring and fall are the periods of the year when most patients are seen. In describing his own series of patients with manic-depressive attacks, Kraines (169) found the time of onset (not the time of hospital admission) to peak twice during the year, in March and September. Lin (199) has related that periodic mania is referred to as "peach-blossom insanity" in Formosa because of the belief that most of the manic episodes occur in the spring when the peach blossoms open. Almost everywhere, the fewest cases of affective disorders are seen during the summer months.

Response to Treatment

Four types of treatment, none of them specific, have been used in depressive disorders: pharmacotherapy, convulsive therapy, psychotherapy, and surgery. To consider them in reverse order of frequency, psychosurgery, introduced in 1937 in the form of prefrontal lobotomy, has been used for some refractory manic-depressive illnesses and severe agitated involutional psychoses in order to reduce the incapacitating severity of the symptoms and the need for repeated hospitalization. It is not considered now except in rare cases.

Psychotherapy is generally thought to be helpful only in situationally induced reactive depression when the objective is to modify the psychologic pattern of response to stress. Supportive psychotherapy offers assistance through reassurance and guidance.

Convulsive therapy, formerly induced by camphor, insulin, and Metrazol, has been used as electric shock therapy since 1938. The mechanism of action of seizure activity in the brain on the depressive disorders is still unknown. Electroconvulsive therapy (ECT) is widely believed to be effective in the treatment of psychotic depressions, particularly of the endogenous type, and ineffective and inadvisable in neurotic depression. It is considered by many to be the treatment of choice in urgently suicidal depressions, since it is said to act more rapidly than any available drugs.

Pharmacotherapy has been the subject of greatest interest and investigation since about 1957, when the newer antidepressant drugs came into experimental and clinical use. Careful examination of seventy-two studies of antidepressant drugs revealed conflicting evidence for therapeutic effectiveness and led Jonathan Cole (54), Chief of the National Institute of Mental Health Psychopharmacology Service Center, to report in 1964 that the place of antidepressants in the physician's armamentarium was not established, although many clinicians felt the drugs were useful and effective. Early in 1967, Cole (55) noted that: "The antidepressants of both the MAO (monamine oxidase inhibitors) and Imipramine types (tricyclic compounds) pose a problem. They generally appear less effective in carefully controlled clinical studies than the experience of many psychiatrists would suggest. In controlled studies, the drugs usually are shown to be better than placebo . . . but not dramatically so."

Lehmann (180) recently reported that of a hospitalized group of 400 to 500 patients with depression, 20 to 25 per cent improved spontaneously in three weeks with no treatment; about 50 per cent improved in the same period of time if given a placebo (which increased the chances of nonspecific response); 60 to 70 per cent improved in three weeks if also given antidepressant drugs; and about 85 per cent improved in three weeks if ECT was added. This is to say that half the hospitalized group improved in three weeks without specific treatment. Lehmann further believes that, if there *is* a response to treatment, only a small part of it can be credited to the therapeutic agent.

Two major factors probably contribute to the inconclusiveness of drug therapy in depression: the capacity of many depressed patients to recover without therapy, in about the period of time required for the drugs to take full effect, and the heterogeneity of the depressive group of illnesses. In addition, the use of psychiatric drugs has by now become so widespread that it may be unrealistic to think of treating an "untreated" individual. Although psychotropic drugs have not yet proved to be very helpful in depression, they are widely used as a research tool in investigations of biochemical abnormalities which may be associated with depression and in the search for diagnostic subgroups of the disorder.

There appears to be a more effective method of treatment for mania. Lithium salts were reported by Cade, in Australia in 1949 (40), to be effective in the treatment of manic excitement, a finding that did not attract much attention until a decade later. Lithium, a common, widely available, inexpensive electrolyte (like sodium), which seems to affect behavior in a predictable and reversible fashion, apparently has been used safely and therapeutically in other countries for some years; it is now under investigation in the United States. Of particular interest are recent reports that lithium may prevent the recurrences so characteristic of some forms of manic-depressive psychosis (12).

The type of treatment received, the place where treatment is given, and the type of therapist available are influenced by the social circumstances and social status of the patients; this has been demonstrated by Hollingshead and Redlich (136) and others. This in turn may influence response to treatment. In Monroe County, New York State, Gardner (98) found that a history of prior hospitalization influenced the patttern of service given to adult outpatients; in all diagnostic categories *except* affective psychosis, patients with prior hospital care had a greater rate of hospitalization than those without such a history. In a comparative study of home and hospital care in two communities in the south of England, Grad and Sainsbury (110) investigated another view, the relative burden on the families of persons with mental illness. In general, relief to families of mentally ill persons was somewhat greater in the hospital-centered service than in the community-care service, for most diagnostic and symptom groups. The only symptom which *significantly* differentiated the relief to families in the two areas was depression. Apparently the persistent hypochondriacal complaints typical of the depressed patients were very troublesome to the families and the constant complaints were not well tolerated under the system of home care.

Although differences in response to treatment of any kind are important features of clinical appraisal and may help to clarify etiology, they must be used with caution to designate a disease entity. The same condition may be mild in some individuals and severe in others, as stressed by Paul Hoch (134). In addition, the same cause may produce widely different clinical pictures and, conversely, the same clinical picture can result from many causes. Kiloh and Garside (162), in a study of the evidence for the independence of neurotic and endogenous depression, apparently ignore such considerations. After describing, incorrectly, a distribution as biomodal and therefore indicating that persons with neurotic and endogenous depression come from two independent groups, they use response to treatment as a final, self-evident discriminator. They state that the dichotomous nature of depressive states is *most* apparent from differential effects of physical treatments, that is, convulsive therapy. In reviewing Roth's (288) series of cases of endogenous and reactive depression in which there was markedly greater improvement among the endogenous cases, Kiloh and Garside state that "if neurotic depression is merely a mild variety of endogenous depression, here then is (an) extraordinary paradox . . . that a mild condition fails to respond to and may even be made worse by a form of treatment that is effective in severe varieties of the same condition!" It may be that these two varieties of depression are distinct, but not for the reason that one responds better than the other to a specific treatment. One may as well say that a primary tuberculous infection is unrelated to cavitary pulmonary tuberculosis because it may not respond to a thoracoplasty, or that valvulotomy for the mitral stenosis of rheumatic heart disease can be conceived of as a useful treatment for streptococcal pharyngitis.

Heredity

Constitutional factors have been studied as inborn characteristics by many investigators, but probably most actively by Kretschmer (174), who described a cycloid type of temperment associated with a pyknic type of constitution (and a schizoid temperament accompanied by an asthenic constitution). About two-thirds of manic-depressive patients were found to have a cycloid temperament and pyknic body build. Sheldon (304) continued this work and concluded that manic-depressives are generally mesomorphs, or a combination of endomorph and mesomorph, with mesomorphic characteristics predominating. A more recent review of the literature (273) failed to reveal any conclusive findings.

Behavior genetics, a union of psychology and genetics, is an expanding field of interest and research encompassing cognitive, social, and personality aspects of human behavior. Psychologic traits may be as likely as most physical traits to be an instrument of genetic selection, in view of the great individual variation observed. Since human behavior is a critical aspect of human adaptation, both hereditary and acquired components may affect certain biologic processes. Lack of knowledge about this effect is partly ascribed to the complexity of the socioeconomic fabric through which most human traits influence human biologic phenomena and to the variability of the biologic phenomena themselves (5).

Early interest in the genetic aspects of the psychoneuroses was shown in the work of Slater (313) and Shields (306). More recently, Gottesman (108) reported a study of normal adolescent twins from the public schools of an urban area in Minnesota, whose personality was assessed by various psychologic tests; their behavioral phenotypes were also described. It was determined that the neuroses with hypochondriacal and hysterical elements had a low genetic component, or none at all, whereas those with elements of anxiety, depression, obsession, and schizoid withdrawal were said to have a substantial genetic component.

The bulk of work on the inheritance of mental disorder has been done in *psychiatric genetics;* it has been based on classical genetic theory and concerned with specific psychoses. Such studies, made in great number and reviewed by various investigators (60, 141), have used three techniques: the familial aggregation or pedigree method, the general population survey method, and the method of twin studies of monozygotic (MZ) and dizygotic (DZ) twins.

Kallmann, who did a great deal of the work in the United States, summarized the relevant morbidity surveys of manic-depressive psychosis reported from Europe and the United States between 1929 and 1950 (153) and concluded that, despite the many diversities among the studies, a marked excess in manic-depressive psychosis among relatives of manic-depressive probands, as compared with the occurrence in the general population, is consistently observed.

Stenstedt (325) conducted a later study in Sweden from 1949 to 1952. This involved 216 manic-depressive patients admitted to psychiatric hospitals during a thirty-year period, 1919-48, from an isolated district with a stable population of approximately 50,000. The investigation covered siblings, parents, children, and spouses, and the total final material comprised 2,325 persons. The diagnosis of manic-depressive psychosis in the probands (90 males and 126 females) was based on the hospital diagnosis of self-limited attacks of mania or depression, with incapacity to work for several months, but without mental deterioration. A similar diagnosis in the 72 secondary cases (36 males and 36 females) was often difficult to make, as information about nonhospitalized or deceased persons had to be obtained from relatives and was frequently not satisfactory. In general, a secondary case was counted as uncertain (43 cases) unless the patient had been treated in the hospital and a case report was available.

The total morbidity risk for manic-depressive psychosis (certain and uncertain cases) in the population of the investigation district was estimated to be about one per cent. The morbidity risks for similar cases among relatives of the study subjects were found to be 14 per cent among siblings, 7.5 per cent among parents, and 17 per cent among children. When the results of previous investigations were considered in conjunction with his study findings, Stenstedt concluded that "it may be assumed that the morbidity risk for manic-depressive psychosis among siblings, as well as among parents and children of manic-depressive probands, is about 15 per cent."

A number of methodologic manipulations were required to arrive at this figure, because several of the morbidity risks were calculated from very small numbers of cases and denominator figures. For example, there were no probands with both parents affected and only twenty-eight with one parent affected. The small group of persons with one parent affected was increased by adding the children of probands "since the children constitute a group of relatives of manic-depressive probands with one affected parent." According to the Weinberg proband method, which was one of the methods used in the study, some probands were counted as secondary cases, so-called "secondary probands," which increased the secondary cases by thirty or forty for some of the computations.

In the consideration of genetic mechanisms it was concluded that manic-depressive psychosis most probably follows a dominant type of inheritance, possibly a simple autosomal dominant gene with incomplete penetrance. The recessive mode of inheritance was ruled out because the frequency of consanguineous marriages between parents of manic-depressives was not increased. The most convincing argument in favor of a dominant type of inheritance (in addition to acceptance of earlier opinions by Slater and Strömgren that "this theory must be shown to be inadequate before any other is even provisionally accepted") was the finding that the morbidity risk for manic-depressive psychosis among parents, siblings, and children was about the same. The fact that the frequency of 15 per cent is far from the 50 per cent that was expected with simple dominant-gene inheritance is ascribed to inhibition of manifestation. Support for the incomplete penetrance hypothesis is derived from a few small studies of manic-depressive twins in which the degree of manifestation was estimated as 50 per cent. The fact that manic-depressive psychosis often occurs in successive generations was seen as support for dominant-gene hypothesis (the skipping of a generation, interpreted as an expression of inhibition of manifestation).

An analysis of the importance of environmental conditions during childhood for the development of manic-depressive psychosis in siblings of probands indicated that unfavorable circumstances may increase the risk, probably because "unfavorable home-conditions may allow an increased manifestation of the genetic basis for manic-depressive psychosis," and also that an unfavorable environment may to some extent be the result of genetic factors in parents which may possibly increase the risk of disease among their children. The role of environmental factors in precipitating the onset of the psychosis was noted but not developed because "It is . . . well known that attacks of manic-depressive psychosis are often unduly attributed to simultaneous environmental difficulties."

This major and carefully conducted study illustrates a widespread tendency in psychiatric genetics to force a fit of poorly defined, heterogeneous syndromes into a simple mendelian single-gene model. Ödegaard points out that differences in marital status alone could result in a significant source of error in studies of the transmission mechanisms of manic-depressive psychosis and schizophrenia. It is said that in the families of manic-depressive probands the parents and the siblings have similar morbidity, whereas in the families of schizophrenic probands, the siblings have much higher morbidity. If one takes into account the frequent reports from other studies that many siblings are unmarried, "the difference disappears and with it the main justification for regarding manic-depressive psychosis as dominant and schizophrenia as recessive" (247).

Some years ago, Pollock and others (264) concluded from their studies in New York State that neither manic-depressive psychosis nor dementia praecox appeared in frequencies compatible with a simple mendelian hypothesis. In St. Louis, during 1961-62, Winokur and Pitts (350) found the patterns of prevalence among relatives of patients with affective disorders to be inconsistent with the hypothesis of either a dominant or a recessive single gene; their methodology, however, does not permit definite conclusions to be made.

Lilienfeld (198) has developed an instructive and amusing example of the methodologic problem of testing a recessive-gene hypothesis. His interest in determining the adequacy of a binomial test in discriminating between genetic and nongenetic factors led to the analysis of data on individual characteristics which occurred with a certain degree of familial aggregation, primarily as a result of nongenetic, social, or environmental conditions. Attendance at a medical school and attendance at the University of Buffalo were the characteristics studied, according to three parental classes: one parent had attended a medical school (or the university); both parents had attended; neither parent had attended. It was found that both attendance at a medical school and attendance at the University of Buffalo were consistent with a recessive type of inheritance. The problems of erroneous inferences drawn from small samples were particularly emphasized.

In a review of twin and twin-family studies of manic-depressive psychosis, Kallmann (154) concluded that all the studies had shown significant differences between the general population and siblings or dizygotic co-twins, and between fraternal and identical twins (see Appendix Table 12). His own twin index-family study in New York State (152) was one of the largest, containing 27 monozygotic and 55 dizygotic pairs with a total of 206 sibs and 16 half-sibs. The essential diagnostic feature was a cyclic illness with acute self-limited mood swings before the fifth decade of life; clearly reactive depressions were excluded. The expectancy of manic-depressive psychosis in relatives was calculated to be 16 per cent for half-sibs, 22 per cent for sibs, 23 per cent for parents, 25 per cent for dizygotic co-twins, and 100 per cent for identical twin partners. Since only patients admitted to a mental hospital were included as affected cases, the concordance rate of 100 per cent for identical twins was interpreted as an artificial maximum value and not an indication of complete penetrance of the genotype. Kallmann, Slater (311, 312), Rosanoff (238), and others have concluded that the genetic basis of the predisposition to endogenous manic-depressive illness is an autosomal dominant gene with incomplete penetrance. (An earlier study by Kallmann and Reisner of tuberculosis in twin index-families, showing the probable role of constitutional factors, yielded strikingly similar ratios, as shown in Appendix Table 13.)

More recent studies of twins have failed to provide more definitive findings; they have, in fact, raised additional questions. Tienari (334) considered all live births in Finland from 1920 to 1929, ascertained same-sexed, male twinships from the birth

HEREDITY

register, and attempted to trace and interview all pairs in which both members were alive and in Finland as of January 1, 1957 (thus reducing the total number of 2,288 pairs by one-half). After elimination of those lost to observation and exclusion of pairs in which one or both members were psychotic or severely mentally deficient (not possible to interview), 252 individuals in 126 pairs of identical twins (zygosity confirmed serologically) remained for study. No affective psychoses were found among the living pairs of identical twins. One case of reactive pyschosis and sixteen cases of schizophrenia were diagnosed. None of the identical co-twins of the schizophrenic patients was diagnosed as schizophrenic. (The five cases of affective illness found among fraternal twins were also discordant.) The case material is small, the study subjects relatively young in age, and the exclusions from the study questionable, but these findings are at complete variance with the earlier twin studies of Slater and Kallmann.

A preliminary report from Munro, in Edinburgh (234), suggests a possible relationship between twinning and depression, on the basis of finding an excess number of twins in a group of hospitalized depressive patients; another study (314) of selected socioenvironmental factors finds no support for the assumption that the environment is the same for both MZ and DZ twins, an assumption important to the genetic explanation of higher intrapair similarity in MZ twins than in DZ twins.

The morbidity risk for schizophrenia among siblings, parents, and children of manic-depressive probands is not different from that in the general population, according to the findings of Kallmann (153) and also of other investigators. Involutional psychosis, which in Kallmann's study included a variety of nonperiodic forms of depressive behavior, agitated anxiety states, and typical cases of involutional melancholia, was not increased in the families of manic-depressives; in fact, involutional psychosis seemed more closely associated genetically with the group of schizoid personality traits than with manic-depressive psychosis. This is at variance with the findings of Stenstedt (326) which suggest that the traditional clinical entity of involutional melancholia is comprised of cases of manic-depressive psychosis and exogenous depression.

Family and population studies of genetic factors must contend with the same problems that other morbidity investigations face: questions of diagnostic criteria, probabilities of accurate case ascertainment, representativeness of samples, small numbers, and adequacy of analytic techniques. Twin studies have the added burdens of accurate determination of zygosity and greater opportunity for unconscious bias. All, however, must come to grips with questions of environmental influences since, in the last analysis, the contribution of hereditary factors is determined by exclusion or specification of the environmental role.

Bradford Hill (131) has said that literally hundreds of disorders or derangements in mankind have been recorded as showing evidence of hereditary factors. This is often based on the appearance of the disability or disease in a more or less orderly fashion among related individuals, as in tuberculosis (75) and pellagra (103). Although in many instances there is no doubt that genetic factors are important, in others the difficult distinction between hereditary and environmental influences must be made. Often, too, notice is taken of only the remarkable cases, without reference to those in which genetic factors are not apparently operant. Even if a reasonably large number of family histories is taken, and if the distribution of multiple cases differs from that expected by chance, the question of a common family environment cannot be ruled out. Rosenthal (286) has cautioned that even when concordance rates are repeatedly higher for monozygotic twins than for dizygotic twins, we cannot be certain that the rates reflect genetic variation.

This is not to say that genetics plays no role in depressive disorder; on the contrary, it appears likely that inherited factors do indeed contribute to etiology. It is simply not yet possible to fit the poorly defined syndromes of the depressive conditions into any known genetic model.

Biochemical and Endocrine Factors

Although no single biochemical defect in mental disease has yet been established, it seems to be the impression among scientists that biochemical abnormalities in the depressive types of mental illness are likely to be among the first to be uncovered. There are three biochemical and endocrine theories of mental depression under current investigation.

Catecholamine Metabolism

In a review of supporting evidence, Schildkraut (296) states that the hypothesis of catecholamine metabolism proposes that some, if not all, depressions are associated with an absolute or relative decrease in catecholamines, particularly norepinephrine, available in various areas of the brain; and, conversely, that elation may be associated with an excess of such amines. Data from pharmacologic studies, mainly in animals, suggest that the actions of both major classes of antidepressant drugs, the monoamine oxidase inhibitors and the imipramine-like agents, are mediated through the catecholamines. By different biochemical mechanisms of action, both of these classes of drugs increase the active catecholamines at receptor sites in the brain. In addition, available evidence suggests that catecholamine depletion is associated with reserpine-induced sedation in animals, although other amines, particularly serotonin, are probably also of importance. Much of the evidence has been inferential from animals to humans, including the most recent work by Schildkraut *et al.*

(297), but more direct methods for human studies are becoming available.

The metabolism of norepinephrine and epinephrine results in two products excreted by the urine; these may be useful as an index of intracellular activity. Bunney and co-workers (37) have reported changes in norepinephrine level in depressed patients which seem to differentiate acute psychotic depression from neurotic depression. They speculate that the possible role of norepinephrine is more complex than simple depletion, but the findings are still inconclusive. Although some of the available data are conflicting, further investigation of the role of norepinephrine apparently has important potential.

Adrenal Hormones

Some of the studies of the relation between behavior and biochemistry in depression have focused on the adrenal hormones, hydrocortisone and cortisol, both of which are related to stress, and both of which break down to 17-hydroxycorticosteroids (17-OHCS), which are excreted in the urine. A significant subgroup of depressions shows increased plasma and urinary levels of 17-OHCS, thus providing an index of adrenal-pituitary activity. Good correspondence is reported between the level of depression and the level of excreted corticosteroids.

Of seventeen depressed patients studied by Bunney *et al.* (39), twelve showed changes in twenty-four-hour urinary 17-OHCS levels which closely paralleled changes in behavior, as rated by a specially trained nursing staff. The closest correlations were found in those patients whose behavior fluctuated the most. On the basis of 17-OHCS levels, two other subgroups were identified. Both subgroups had high depression ratings, but the 17-OHCS levels of one were within or below normal range, while the other showed levels two to three times normal or higher. The most prominent behavioral differences between these two subgroups were seen in their awareness of and struggle with their illness. Patients in the high-level groups seemed to have no effective defenses against their thoughts of guilt and death, whereas those with low 17-OHCS levels showed intense denial of their illness, even when severe depressive symptoms were apparent.

Bunney's group hypothesized that high 17-OHCS levels reflect what they call "psychic distress or pain." Denial, they say, may be a defense mechanism which prevents the depressed person from fully experiencing the intense pain and turmoil indicated by his behavior. An illustration of this concept was provided by a study of a patient with regular forty-eight-hour manic-depressive cycles which persisted with clocklike regularity over a period of two years (38). Urinary 17-OHCS levels were low on a manic day, rose sharply on the depressed day that followed, and then dropped again the next day. The patient's manic defenses included marked denial of illness, periodic amnesia, and little or no awareness of the feelings of guilt, suffering, and hopelessness that were so prominent during her depressed days. During the manic phases, even though her behavior was combative and she appeared to be in an intense panic, her 17-OHCS levels remained low. This observation does not fit the traditional concepts of response to stress, and the investigators suggest that they may offer a biochemical confirmation of the theory that mania is a defense against the pain of depression.

It is not known whether the mechanisms underlying altered adrenal function in depression are general or specific. Much depression has been reported in Cushing's syndrome, as well as suicide, and depression has also been noted in Addison's disease. Coppen (58) believes that although there is evidence that cortisol can alter mood, the adrenocortical changes are not of primary importance in most cases of affective disorders.

Electrolyte Metabolism

Recent investigations on electrolyte metabolism by Coppen *et al.* (59) have demonstrated changes in the distribution of body water and electrolytes in mania and depression. A significant increase in residual sodium (probably mainly intracellular sodium) in depression, and a very marked increase in residual sodium in mania, together with a decrease in extracellular water, have been reported. There is also a reduction in intracellular potassium. The etiologic significance of these changes is not clear, nor are the factors which can produce such a profound alteration in the distribution of electrolytes (56). Radioactive isotope dilution techniques now make possible a more direct approach to the estimation of intracellular sodium and potassium. Lithium, which takes the place of sodium, and has been found to be effective in the treatment of manic behavior, may also offer a promising research tool for the study of mania and depression.

The question of whether these three systems may be a cause or a result of behavior and emotional states remains, of course, to be answered. Kety (161) believes these theories are important but are still in the general, rather than the specific, realm of association with affective disorders. In noting the enormous complexity of interrelationships in behavior patterns, he suggests that although chemical mechanisms may possibly be responsible for the *intensity* of affect, no simplistic model of affective disorder, in biochemical terms or any others, can be adequate.

Manic-Depressive Link

It has been said that the manic-depressive type of disorder is the only psychosis whose chief features may be unequivocally recognized down through the ages (147). Kraepelin's view of mania and depression as a single morbid process was based in large measure on the striking and characteristic tendency toward change and replacement from one state to the other in the same individual. Cameron (41) also postulated that elation and depression are not fundamentally opposed metabolic processes, because various physiologic and biochemical comparisons did not differentiate the two moods. The same alternating manic and depressive phases did not represent to Zilboorg (355) a separate clinical entity but rather a pure form of a cyclical rhythm easily observed in other mental disturbances such as hysteria, compulsion neuroses, and even various forms of schizophrenia. Many other observations have been made on cyclic and periodic phenomena (74, 226).

Frank (93) has taken the position that it is misleading and confusing to consider the depression-elation response in association with manic-depressive psychosis. The evidence "indicates that depression-elation forms part of a system maintained in a state of dynamic equilibrium, in many ways like that of sleeping and waking." He notes that this biologic mechanism has received little study, despite the voluminous literature on manic-depressive psychosis, possibly because it does not lend itself to animal experimentation, as do the more acute, shorter biologic responses connected with hunger, pain, fear, and rage. His thesis is that depression-elation responses constitute part of the inherent adaptive machinery available to the individual. They are used automatically, unconsciously, and directly as adaptive mechanisms under conditions in which, in actuality or fantasy, a relatively helpless individual is threatened with the loss of suitable care, protection, and sustenance. He believes the coordinated machinery for the depression-elation responses exists side by side with the rage, anxiety, and sexual reactions, and has, as they do, survival value. The patterning is biologic but the use the individual makes of these available devices becomes increasingly a matter of his life experience and, thereby, of his psychology.

The depression-elation pattern can come into play when very basic metabolic functions are being poorly maintained or are threatened, whether the threat is actual or imagined, and can go in the direction of either increased or decreased activity. On occasion, the depression-elation machinery is set into action in anticipation of danger, in contrast to its use as part of mourning where it represents a response to a loss that has already occurred. There is also clinical evidence of the interrelationship of biologic cyclic changes with depression-elation responses, like that seen during menstruation and menopause, and after childbirth.

Frank speculates that some stereotyped behavioral reactions may represent primitive responses whose use we rationalize in psychologic terms. Preoccupation with the mood changes has made it difficult to think in terms of organized adaptive depressive-elative responses.

An even more primitive biologic mechanism has been postulated by Curt Richter (278) in terms of biologic clocks. Richter makes the distinction between the many devices that maintain various conditions of the body at fixed levels (the "fixity of the internal environment" of Claude Bernard and the "homeostasis" of Walter Cannon) and the more ancient timing devices, biologic clocks, which exert control over functions and behavior of the whole organism in the *complete absence* of any homeostatic control or any feedback from the organs or autonomic, emotional, and mental functions which they regulate: "as independent of the rest of the organism as a wrist watch is of its wearer." These innate hypothalamic clocks or timing devices, whose existence in humans is hypothesized on the basis of careful animal work, function unnoticeably in conditions of physical and mental health. Their existence becomes known only when, in the course of an illness, synchronization of the clocks goes awry and all the timing devices are in phase, resulting in almost precise twenty-four-hour cyclic manifestations.

Such cyclic phenomena make their appearance during illnesses of various kinds, but in no more than a small group of patients —perhaps three or four per cent of manic-depressives or schizophrenics. These phenomena have sharp onsets of two daily phases, occur with a high degree of accuracy at the same time each day, have a high degree of constancy of alternation for years, and may persist for as long as thirty years independently of all external and internal conditions or disturbances. They appear to be periodic manifestations of basic illnesses rather than periodic diseases, since they make their appearance in humans long after the start of the basic illness. The periodicity seems incidental to the basic pathology, since therapeutic elimination of the cycle does not eliminate the disease, although it improves outlook and function.

Of special interest are patients with manic-depressive disease who exhibit forty-eight-hour clock mechanisms, such as a depressed patient who goes into a much deeper depression and becomes suicidal in one twenty-four-hour phase and is nearly normal in the next (278), and other examples cited by Bunney and associates (38). A recent report by Jenner *et al.* (148) describes a man who in his forties began to show an almost precise forty-eight-hour cycle of changing mood. He was elated and overactive for twenty-four hours, depressed and lethargic for the next twenty-four hours, then again elated, and so on; this condition persisted for eleven years. The physiologic variables studied were inconclusive from an etiologic viewpoint; the investigators feel that external diurnal factors which may determine the rhythm must be separated from those that cause the disease.

Association with Physical Conditions

In general, there is a widely accepted distinction between two broad types of mental disorders, those accompanying a known organic or physical condition and those occurring in the absence of known physical factors. The mental complications of physical illness are seen infrequently by psychiatrists because they are generally considered to belong in the general field of medicine. Mayer-Gross and colleagues (220) have expressed regret at the virtual disappearance of this interest because they feel that careful and critical clinical observations can add to our knowledge. Little is known about the frequency of severe mental symptoms in somatic illness, and "the mild (symptoms) escape the psychiatrist and are ignored by the physician and surgeon."

Much work has been done on the association between physical and emotional disturbance in psychophysiologic disorders, somatization reactions, organ neuroses, and psychosomatic illnesses. In general morbidity studies, persons classed as psychoneurotic (and their families) have been outstanding because of their experience of illness in all categories (respiratory illness, accidental injuries, and all other acute illnesses); psychoneurotic persons have appeared to be especially susceptible to the development of certain conditions such as hypertensive vascular disease, at relatively early ages (71).

Although depression has been observed in almost all types of illnesses and disturbances, whether infectious, metabolic, endocrine, toxic, malignant, degenerative, or traumatic, very little is known about the frequency or significance of such relationships. In a condition such as anorexia nervosa, for example, a type of morbid fasting that has many depressive features, it has not been possible to make clear-cut associations.

In 1928, Ewald (89) reported a series of 124 cases of influenza psychoses from the literature in which 40 per cent showed depressive or neurasthenic states. In studies of symptom complaints of psychiatric interest reported by general practitioners in two "new towns" in the environs of London (331), high one-year prevalence rates for the depressed states were partially explained by a preceding severe influenza epidemic with its resultant depression, lassitude, and debility. Depression and even suicide are said to be a rather frequent complication of infectious hepatitis and depression has been frequently described in infectious mononucleosis. In outbreaks of benign myalgic encephalomyelitis (Iceland disease), a polio-like disease first described in 1934, mental symptoms including depression are a striking feature of the acute, convalescent, and relapse stages. Some of the depressions are severe enough to require hospitalization and convulsive therapy, and one has led to suicide (4).

Mental symptoms may antedate the physical signs of pellagra by weeks or months, in the form of neurasthenia, often accompanied by depression and suicidal tendencies. Electrolyte disturbances, notably potassium deficiency, from maintenance on potassium-free intravenous fluids or as a result of dietary deficiencies, may frequently lead to depression which is sometimes profound and associated with suicidal thoughts (220). Extrapyramidal disturbance, particularly spasmodic torticollis, has been associated with depression and suicide (64), and patients with prolonged facial pain have been found to have had a background of depressive illness (177). It has been suggested that severe depressive reactions may occur with diminished frequency among retarded adults (101).

Endocrine disorders have traditionally been linked with emotional disturbance, but specific association is yet to be established. Much psychiatric disturbance is reported in Cushing's syndrome (excessive production of cortisol), almost always as a depressive mood, although occasionally there is some hyperactivity; depressive psychosis has been reported in almost 20 per cent of one series of cases. In Addison's disease (adrenocortical insufficiency), depression was noted in one fourth of a series of cases, and euphoria in one half. Hypopituitarism (chronic anterior pituitary failure) has also been associated with depression and apathy, as well as other psychiatric symptoms (228).

Drug-induced depression was reported when reserpine was first used in the treatment of hypertension. More recently the phenothiazines have been implicated, although it has been said that careful investigation of depressions following the use of phenothiazines reveals a history of psychic and environmental stresses. Reactions to cortisone and benzedrine have been described as manic-like in some cases (18).

"Separation and depression" have been reported as a precipitating factor in a wide variety of medical disorders (298). Illnesses such as ulcerative colitis, rheumatoid arthritis, leukemia, and osteoarthritis have been precipitated by bereavement, according to numerous reports; depression has been suggested to be a contributing factor in the development of pernicious anemia (191). In outcome studies of myocardial infarction, it has been reported that there is an increased risk of dying if the individual is a depressive as judged by the MMPI-D scale (178).

Early Development

Dubos and co-workers (76) have written a paper on biologic Freudianism in which they note that the phrase "early influences," as commonly used, denotes the conditioning of behavior by the experiences of very early life. They point out that early environmental experiences do more than condition behavioral patterns; they also affect profoundly, and often lastingly, many biologic characteristics of the adult. A report from The Johns Hopkins Hospital (265) illustrates this with a description of profound growth disturbance resembling dwarfism in thirteen children who had come from severely abnormal home environments (and their remarkable growth after admission to the hospital). One may add that the even earlier experiences of intrauterine life also play a role in the mental and physical development of the individual, as suggested by the experiments on auditory imprinting in prenatal life, reported by Salk (294), and the relation between abnormalities of the prenatal period and behavior disorders in children, described by Rogers and others (282). The reciprocal situation also deserves attention; the characteristics of the newborn infant influence behavior toward him, and thereby affect his environment in early childhood.

The influence of various types of childhood experiences on personality development and on the appearance of behavior and psychiatric disturbances has been the subject of an immense amount of investigation and speculation. Because the associations are manifold and extraordinarily complex, and the methodologic problems are great, few generalizations can be drawn. A careful and balanced reassessment of the effects of deprivation of maternal care (352) concluded that maternal deprivation does indeed have an adverse effect on development both during and after the deprivation experience, and that severe experiences can lead in some cases to grave, irreversible effects. ". . . These adverse effects, however, differ in nature, severity and duration, and these differences are themselves related to qualitative and quantitative differences in the deprivation experience . . . much further research is required before the relationship between antecedent depriving conditions and their effects can be specified in detail." There has been far less research on paternal deprivation or its interaction with maternal loss or separation.

With respect to depression, two general types of investigation have been made, those concerned with the occurrence of depression in the early years, and those relating childhood bereavement to adult depression.

Spitz (317) described infant depression and distinguished critical time periods in the development of depression in emotionally deprived institutionalized infants which influenced the reversibility of the condition. If severe emotional deprivation lasted no longer than about three months during the first year and a half of life, the effects appeared to be reversible by renewal of contact with the mother; if it lasted longer than about five months, the process of emotional and physical deterioration progressed, became self-perpetuating, and frequently led to death. In general, the effects of deprivation were most traumatic when the mother-child relationship was good; they occurred far less frequently when the relationship was very poor from the start.

Bowlby (31) has come to interpret the behavior of young children deprived of maternal care as that of childhood mourning and has described the mood as a depressive one. The sequence that follows separation involves first protest and anxiety with crying, and then despair with apathy and fading hope of reunion, and finally detachment from the maternal bond with impoverishment of affection. These steps are observed in the basic mourning process at any age but are greatly accelerated in the young child. The intensity and prematurity of onset of the defensive processes, with resulting fixation, explains why experiences of loss in early childhood may lead to faulty personality and proneness to mental illness. If separation lasts for more than six months or if separations have been repeated, so that the child is in an advanced stage of detachment, the process may be irreversible and the child may remain detached and never recover his affection for his parents. The processes of mourning in childhood, Bowlby believes, always take a course that in adults is considered pathologic. In Keeler's view (159), children's reactions to the death of a parent simulated both the normal and the pathologic states of mourning seen in adults.

An exceptional opportunity to conduct an "experiment of nature" on infant depression was reported by Engel and co-workers (82, 83). A child, Monica, born in 1952 with atresia of the esophagus and sent home after corrective surgery, was readmitted at age fifteen months, cachetic and depressed. Close observation showed that: "After recovery from the depression and the marasmic state . . . a striking behavior pattern was encountered which (was) called the depressive-withdrawal reaction. This reaction typically occurred when the infant was confronted alone by a stranger and was characterized by muscular inactivity, hypotonia, and a sad facial expression, decreased gastric secretion and eventually a sleep state. It vanished as soon as the baby was reunited with a familiar person . . . a depressive reaction which could be provoked and terminated at will." The phenomena of reduced activity and reduced interaction with the environment were, in the opinion of the investigators, an integral part of the biologic depression pattern and, possibly, the anlage of later depression.

In a study of a group of older children and adolescents who attempted suicide, Lourie (205) did not find a clinical picture dominated by depressive thinking. He stressed, however, the importance of patterns of thinking, relationships, and impulse control which originate in the first few years of life and continue into adolescence when developmental crises may occur. Similar conclusions have been reported by Jacobs and Teicher (145).

Studies of the role of parental deprivation in the development of adult depression have been inconclusive. Gregory, who critically reviewed past studies of childhood bereavement in various types of mental disorder (113), made comparisons with parental loss in general population groups (114), and used clinical diagnoses and MMPI ratings (115), has not been able to demonstrate a significant association between parental loss and any of the psychiatric diagnostic groups. Pitts and colleagues (259) also failed to find a relationship in their patients in St. Louis.

In Hampstead, England, Brown (34) found that childhood bereavement was significantly higher in depressive patients than it was in general practice and hospital patients and in the general population. The loss of mothers was significant throughout childhood up to age fifteen, whereas the loss of fathers was more significant in the later childhood years, five through fourteen. Patients who were sufficiently depressed to be referred by their general practitioners to the outpatient department of the local general hospital over a five-year period, 1955-60, were the study subjects. There were 61 males and 155 females, a total of 216 patients who were in the main mildly depressed. Controls were 267 general practice and medical-surgical hospital patients. The 1921 census estimates for orphans were used for the general population figures. An extension of this work (35) again showed a significant proportion of maternal and paternal deaths before the age of fifteen in future depressives.

Similar findings from Britain have been reported by Dennehy (66), who found the loss of father in the age group from ten to fifteen most marked. Hill and Price (132) compared depressed psychiatric inpatients with nondepressed psychiatric inpatients and also found paternal bereavement at the years between ten and fourteen the most striking, with no difference in maternal loss. Munro (235) found that depressives as a group are more likely than normal persons to have lost a father by death during the age period between eleven and fifteen, and that severe depressives are more likely to have lost a mother during their childhood.

In Philadelphia, Beck *et al.* (18) studied 297 psychiatric outpatients and inpatients according to severity of depression, as judged by a depression inventory. They found that loss of father had occurred more frequently than loss of mother for patients of both sexes in all levels of depression. There was a significantly greater incidence of loss of a parent before age sixteen in the severely depressed compared with the nondepressed group; this association was not evident when the usual nosologic categories of depression were used.

Stenstedt, in the course of his study of genetic factors in manic-depressive illness, made an analysis of the influence of environmental conditions in childhood (325). The dissolution of the family before the child was fifteen years old was a notable factor in increasing the risk of psychosis among siblings of the cases.

An epidemiologic study of precursors of various chronic diseases offered Paffenbarger and Asnes (254) the opportunity to investigate characteristics possibly associated with future suicides. The college records of 40,000 male, former students, enrolled between 1926 and 1950 at the University of Pennsylvania and Harvard were analyzed; 225 suicides were identified by early 1965. For each suicide, two control subjects, known to be still alive, were randomly chosen from the same school and year. It was found that significantly more suicides than controls had reported at the time of college entrance that their father was dead, while the frequency of maternal deaths was alike for both groups.

In all of these studies, there are differences in diagnostic criteria, types of populations studied, and concepts of deprivation which make comparisons difficult between one study and another. Most troublesome, however, are the unsettled questions of suitable control groups, and appropriate experiences for comparison with the study groups.

Psychodynamics

For the purpose of this review, no attempt will be made to present the many, often differing, psychoanalytic concepts of depression. A comprehensive and critical review in 1960 by

Mendelson (223) delineated the pattern of historical development that has led to "the present still imperfect understanding of this problem." Mendelson lauded Abraham, Freud, Rado, Gero, Melanie Klein, Bibring, Edith Jacobson, and Mabel Blake Cohen and her colleagues as the psychoanalytic workers who have contributed most to the theory on depression.

Abraham (1), a pupil of Freud's, introduced manic-depressive psychosis into the field of psychoanalysis and postulated that manic and depressive phases are dominated by the same complexes: the depressive is defeated by them, the manic ignores and denies them. He thought melancholia was a regression to the oral level of libido and that in the free intervals between episodes of manic-depressive illness the manic-depressive is an obsessional neurotic. He compared melancholic depression with normal grief, a concept that Freud developed in a classic paper, "Mourning and Melancholia," in 1917 (95). Freud's formulations are presented in some detail because of their importance for and influence on all subsequent work.

In his effort to shed light on the nature of melancholia through an analysis of the normal emotion of grief, Freud warned against having too great expectations, because the definition of melancholia, even in descriptive psychiatry, was uncertain; the various clinical forms of melancholia, some of which suggested somatic rather than psychogenic afflictions, did not warrant a unified theory. On the basis of cases in which the psychogenic nature of melancholia was indisputable, he felt a correlation between melancholia and mourning was justified by the general picture of the two conditions.

He described mourning as the regularly occurring grief reaction to the loss of a loved person or an abstraction which has taken the place of one, such as an ideological belief. He drew particular attention to the fact that although grief involves grave departures from the normal attitude to life, it never occurs to us to regard it as a morbid condition and to advise medical treatment, since we are certain it will be overcome after a lapse of time, and, in fact, we regard any interference with it as inadvisable and even harmful. This attitude has been reinforced more recently by Lindemann (202, 203).

Melancholia, too, may be the reaction to the loss of a loved object or ideal. It may also develop, however, when a loss appears to have been experienced, but it is difficult to perceive what it is that has been lost. This suggests that melancholia is in some ways related to an unconscious loss of a love-object, in contradistinction to mourning, in which there is nothing unconscious about the loss.

The distinguishing mental features of melancholia were described by Freud as being the same as those of grief, with one notable exception. In both, there is a profoundly painful dejection, abrogation of interest in the outside world, loss of the capacity to love, and inhibition of all activity. The exception is the fall in self-esteem which occurs in melancholia, the lowering of feelings of self-regard to a degree that leads to self-reproach and culminates in a delusional expectation of punishment.

In grief, the world becomes poor and empty; in melancholia, it is the ego itself that is impoverished. The melancholic represents himself as worthless, reproaches himself for past as well as present uselessness, and completes this delusional belittling, which is predominantly moral, by sleeplessness, refusal of nourishment, and abandonment of the instinct to survive. Dissatisfaction with the self on moral grounds is the most outstanding clinical feature of melancholia; much less frequently, self-criticism concerns itself with bodily infirmity, ugliness, or social inferiority. In analytic terms, however, the self-reproaches are seen to be reproaches against a loved object which have been shifted to the patient's own ego—a narcissistic identification of the ego with the abandoned love-object.

The occasions giving rise to melancholia for the most part extend beyond the clear case of a loss by death, and include all the situations in which one is wounded, hurt, neglected, out of favor, or disappointed; these can impart opposite feelings of love and hate into the relationship or reinforce an already existing ambivalence. This conflict of ambivalence, the origin of which may be partly experiential and partly constitutional, is an important conditioning factor in melancholia.

Melancholia shares another feature with grief in the way it passes off after a certain period of time has elapsed without leaving any gross change. In grief, this time is necessary to carry out the detailed step-by-step testing of reality, thereby making it possible for the ego to free itself from the lost object. Perhaps an analogous situation holds for the course of a melancholia. The sleeplessness characteristic of melancholia evidently testifies to the inflexibility of the condition; the complex of melancholia "behaves like an open wound." It draws to itself energy from all sides, depleting the ego, and is easily able to withstand the ego's wish to sleep. The amelioration of the depression that is regularly noticeable toward evening is probably due to a somatic factor and not explicable psychologically.

The most remarkable peculiarity of melancholia for psychodynamics, and the one most in need of explanation in Freud's view, is the tendency it displays to turn into a mania accompanied by a completely opposite symptomatology. From the psychoanalytic standpoint, the content of mania is no different from that of melancholia. Both disorders wrestle with the same "complex"; in melancholia the ego has succumbed to it, whereas in mania it has mastered the complex and thrust it aside. Another view postulates that all states of triumph and exaltation, which form the normal counterparts of mania, are conditioned the same way. First, there is a long-sustained state of great mental expenditure; then, some influence makes it superfluous; and finally, the large volume of energy becomes available for other ways of application and discharge. Alcoholic intoxication was seen as belonging to the same group of conditions and was explained in the same way, insofar as it consisted in a state of elation.

These speculations about the mechanism of mania were regarded by Freud as indefinite and inadequate. He asked why normal grief is not followed by a manic period (as a matter of fact, it sometimes is; families have been known to be hilarious at meals following funerals, as an example). He suggested at a later date that the mood swings of normal and neurotic persons are caused by the tensions between ego and ego ideal. These mood swings are excessive in the case of manic-depressive illness, and the manic phase represents a triumphant reunion between ego and ego ideal, but not in the sense of a stabilized equilibrium.

In both melancholia and obsessional neurosis, the sufferers usually succeed in the end in taking revenge on the original objects, by the circuitous path of self-punishment, and in tormenting them by means of the illness, having developed the latter so as to avoid the necessity of openly expressing their hostility against the loved ones. It is this sadism, and only this, Freud stated, that solves the riddle of the tendency to suicide which makes melancholia so interesting, and so dangerous. The analysis of melancholia shows that the ego can kill itself only when it is able to launch against itself the animosity relating to an object. In the two contrasting situations of intense love and of suicide, the ego is overwhelmed by the object, though in totally different ways.

Rado (269) extended and recast the theory of depression into the framework of the divided personality which Freud had conceived (an id, ego, and superego, each part having its specific derivation, aims, and mode of functioning). Rado emphasized the desperate need for love in melancholics and formulated the sequence of fear, guilt, atonement, and forgiveness which attempts to recapitulate the infant's experience of rage, hunger, feeding, and satisfaction. He viewed depression as a process of miscarried repair: the opposite of a healthy reaction to serious loss which involves calming the emotions, marshaling resources, and increasing adaptive efficiency. The repair process of the melancholic invokes the obsolete adaptive pattern of alimentary maternal dependence and by this regressive move incapacitates the individual still more.

In Rado's theory, suicide appeared to be "a superlative bid for forgiveness" based on the illusion that this will gain nourishing, loving maternal support forever. The obsessional character (and occasional paranoid pattern) of the depressive in remission was seen as a defense mechanism to drain off aggressive impulses into social channels; it tends to disappear during a depressive spell. The manic phase was an unstable reconciliation reached through denial of guilt. Neurotic depression and true melancholia were seen as similar, except that in neurosis the reparative struggle involves the real object as well as the one in the psychic sphere.

Bibring (23), who believed that all depression results from conflict within the ego itself rather than between ego and superego, has put emphasis on the loss of self-esteem as the cardinal feature of affective disorders. He summed up all the features that different kinds of depression have in common, including not only the depressions of circular psychosis but also the reactive depressions and depressions that occur in the course of physical illness and in states of fatigue or exhaustion. A common feature is the lowering of self-esteem (the loss of self-love which in melancholia is intensified into self-hate). While this may result from early childhood deprivation of love, predisposing to future depression, self-esteem may also be diminished by frustration of other aspirations and at other times. Bibring compared depression with states of depersonalization and boredom.

Frank (93) compared nonspecific depressions to the hibernation of animals, a defensive response to frustrating life conditions. Depression tones down desires and expectations so that the shock of unavoidable frustration is reduced to a minimum. Lewin (190) regarded elation as an important defense mechanism of denial against depression. He compared mania to the dream of a small child, in its fantasy wish fulfillment.

Melanie Klein, the controversial leader of the "English School" of psychoanalysis, postulated that many of the psychic developments described by Freud as occurring later in childhood occur in fact in early infancy (164, 165). She believed that from earliest infancy on there is an interaction between internal and external factors in the development of object relations, of the superego, and of the sense of guilt. She described regularly occurring fixation points in early infancy, called the paranoid position and the depressive position. The paranoid position (phase) develops first as an automatic defense against pain or displeasure in the form of projection. The depressive position (phase) follows, at about the time of weaning, after the mother is first recognized as being one person, the same person who is at times gratifying and at other times depriving, both good and bad. An excess of bad experience leads to inner conflict which characterizes the depressive position, and the first guilt feelings arise as predecessors of what is subsequently conscience formation. All children go through these transitory phases. In manic-depressive psychosis and in mourning there is regression to these early patterns of unsuccessful integration.

Her hypothesis has been used to explain similarities between infantile and psychotic states of mind. Spitz feels that she has mistakenly elevated a pathologic process to the level of a central physiologic process. Anna Freud (94) points out that although Klein had always included children with severe ego defects and psychoses among her patients, she had drawn inferences about normal infantile development from her investigations.

It has been suggested by Hoffer (135) that the depressive mood in the child is at the start an exhaustion phenomenon, with no meaning for the child, a signal that other forms of appeal, such as crying, have failed. If the signal quality is understood and responded to, the child may learn to use the depressive mood as an appeal to arouse attention; that is, the biologic depression pattern may lead to the psychic use of depression as a distress signal. Since active response to an internal danger seems impossible in depression, this may be the way to overcome the feeling of hopelessness and use it for survival. The occurrence of depression as a psychic phenomenon, rather than merely as a physical condition, implies at least the early emergence of the ego, according to Greenacre, who has seen infants in the pre-verbal period with well marked cycles of mood.

Aggression was formerly regarded as central to the development of depression; now it is viewed by some as secondary to the loss of self-esteem, and others believe the hostility shown by the patient may be due to his annoying impact upon others, rather than to primary motivation to do injury to them. In an intensive study of the interpersonal and familial environments of twelve manic-depressive patients, Cohen and colleagues (51) observed that the guilt expressed by the depressive does not carry on to any genuine feeling of regret or effort to change behavior. It is, rather, a means to an end; merely displaying feelings of guilt is expected to suffice for regaining approval. This possibly stems from a feeling that a secure, human relationship with authority can never be achieved.

Feelings of guilt have been prominently and consistently associated with depression for a very long time. This association is doubly interesting because of its extension to cultural interpretations such as the designation of Western societies as guilt cultures (and simpler societies, relatively free of guilt, as shame cultures). Interpretations of guilt and shame, from a psychoanalytic and a cultural viewpoint, have been made by Piers and Singer (258).

In both theory and practice, psychiatric concern is with the *feeling of guilt* in the individual, not the guilt itself. Early clinical psychiatry looked on the highly developed feeling of guilt and its associated self-punishing self-reproach as a characteristic of melancholics. Through psychoanalysis, guilt feelings are seen as neurotic phenomena, the consequences of distorted developmental ambivalences, inevitable and in some measure ineradicable. Development of the sense of guilt is generally thought to be bound up with the superego. According to Freud, when the Oedipus complex declines, the parents of the young child become an admonishing and prohibiting agency, and then guilt and the manifestations of conscience appear.

At first, guilt is hardly distinguishable from fear. The fear from which it seems to arise, and which may always remain an integral part of it, is a fear of the unpleasant consequences of not acting in accordance with certain admonitions. Originally, these consequences were external punishment and loss of parental love. Later on, they develop into a purely internal sense of sin, unworthiness or self-dissatisfaction, in accordance with the development of the superego. The most extreme degree of loss of self-esteem is a feeling of psychic annihilation, like that seen in cases of melancholia. The sense of terrifying frustration corresponds to a child's fear that, as a result of its own primitive desires and aggressions, all sources of satisfaction and relief of tension may be permanently and totally removed. The origin of neurotic guilt may be a very primitive biologic pattern, as was suggested at an international symposium on the genesis of guilt (142). Just as certain animals, caught in a life-endangering situation, may sacrifice parts of themselves in order to survive, so the human being may undertake a sort of biologic self-mutilation on a psychic level.

The distinction between *guilt* and *guilt feelings* has been stressed, particularly by the existentialists. Buber (36), believed that guilt and also conscience are primal qualities of the human race. It is in the nature of man that he can become guilty and know it; there exists real, existential, personal guilt, fundamentally different from psychic guilt feelings or legal or collective or theologic guilt. Guilt as a reality, in the relation between a person and the world entrusted to him in his life, occurs when someone injures another. This type of authentic guilt is not an exception, in Buber's opinion; it is very often inextricably mixed with the problematic, the "neurotic," the "groundless" guilt. He believes the guilt *feeling* can hardly ever be wholly traced to a transgression against a taboo of a family or society. The depth of the guilt feeling is often connected with just that part of the guilt that cannot be ascribed to taboo offense, hence with existential guilt.

Authentic guilt cannot be comprehended through repression or reaching consciousness; the bearer of this guilt remembers it again and again by himself. Psychotherapists do not concern themselves with the real, unrepressed, remembered guilt feelings, the inner consequences of man's betrayal of a friend or a cause. For their patients, "it is a great relief to be diverted from their authentic guilt feelings to an ambiguous neurotic one that allows itself to be discovered in dreams or free association." With the silencing of guilt feelings through psychoanalysis there can be improvement and good functioning, but not personal fulfillment. Buber's contention is that psychology and psychotherapy should be concerned with the real events of guilt as well as the psychic "projection" of guilt.

Whether a sense of guilt is innate or acquired remains an unanswered question. One view is that we begin with a norm or conscience or sense of culpability, but we tend to get morbid deviations from it; another is that the sense of guilt begins in a more primitive way and that the development into a normal conscience is a long process. Freud had suggested a sense of guilt was connected with a primary masochism. Others believe that it proceeds from incorporation into the person of the parental condemnation and punishment, which, having been absorbed, remain as a sense of guilt.

Gottschalk (109) discusses the many difficulties of adequate testing of psychodynamic hypotheses and notes the lack of enthusiasm of psychologic test constructors to develop quantitative measures of such items as separation anxiety, "shame" versus "guilt," anxiety about submissiveness or dependence, inward hostility or suppressed resentment, and "depression proneness." He believes interdisciplinary collaboration is needed and that it can open up additional avenues of investigation.

V

PERSPECTIVES FOR FUTURE RESEARCH

Depression has been characterized as a feeling, a reaction, a syndrome, and an illness. Depression as a feeling is known to everyone under ordinary conditions of life and loss, and is a component in the symptom complex of most, if not all, indispositions and illnesses, as well as almost all mental disturbances. It has been called the common cold of psychiatric practice. The range of depression, from feeling to illness, from transient sadness to persistent melancholia, is a gradient of severity and duration of the depressive mood. Whether it is also a spectrum of *clinical* severity is not known, since diagnostic criteria are poorly defined.

Depressions are mood disturbances. They vary greatly in

symptomatic intensity; they take many clinical forms; they respond to available therapeutic remedies in a nonspecific way, if at all; and they vary in outcome over a vast spectrum from spontaneous recovery to self-destruction. Their etiology remains obscure. Knowledge and theory about them have not advanced very much beyond the level of clinical description.

The epidemiology of depressive states has been only slightly explored. More often than not, depressions have been studied, or merely enumerated, as part of the total group of mental disorders. The principal medium for investigation has been the morbidity survey. Hypotheses about the nature, course, and consequences of depression which have emerged have remained largely untested.

It has not been the obvious problem of diagnosis and classification in mental disturbance that has limited the extent of epidemiologic effort; a surprisingly large volume of work has been done with specified case criteria. It is, rather, the narrowness of range of the effort and objectives. Although there can be no doubt that great gaps in knowledge and theory impose serious limitations on the range of epidemiologic research, they do not preclude a varied (274) but systematic search for new knowledge. Indeed, it is by the very pursuit of tentative and suggestive hypotheses to the point of elimination or continued study that clues may be found to more sophisticated penetrations.

From this review, it seems that the epidemiology of depressive conditions should be studied separately from that of mental disorders as a group. There are two reasons for this: the problems of all mental disorders or all psychoses or all neuroses are too vast to be approached effectively, regardless of shared characteristics; and the differences so far described between depressions and other mental disorders (notably schizophrenia), in important nonclinical as well as clinical features, are sufficiently impressive to warrant independent investigation. Several possible study approaches suggest themselves.

Natural History. A major obstacle to the study of the natural history of depressions has been the absence of end points (the lack of standard events which can be used for objective study and comparison). There appear to be two events which can be specified with relative certainty and which need not be subject to wide differences in concepts and practices: recurrences and deaths by suicide.

Recurrences of depressive or manic-depressive episodes are considered by many to be so characteristic of one type of depressive illness, the manic-depressive type of psychosis, that this diagnosis is rarely made at the time of the initial episode unless there are other circumstances that are regarded as compelling. Whether the number, frequency, or clinical features of episodes of illness are characteristic of a specific type of depressive disorder is not known and it is not clear whether such periodic manifestations have any etiologic or prognostic significance.

Suicide as an outcome of depressions warrants careful investigation because of the strong association between depressive illness and self-inflicted death. Whether this is related to specific types of depressions or represents a possible consequence of depressive illness in general is not known. If mortality by suicide is an additional dimension to the natural history of depressive disorders, it offers a definitive outcome event for depression research.

Study of the survivorship experience of persons with depressions, and of the experience of an appropriate group without depressive illness, can make possible a comparison of characteristics of survivors and nonsurvivors and a study of factors possibly related to suicide. The many large follow-up studies of manic-depressive disease that were reported, particularly in earlier years, are notable for their careful clinical observations but are less meticulous about time periods of observation, losses to follow-up, methods of analysis, and other considerations necessary to reliable longitudinal studies. Possibly, a re-examination of the case material of some of these studies, with the investigators themselves when this is possible, may yield crude working estimates of fatality rates from suicide.

Prospective studies. Etiologic hypotheses about depression are not ready for testing by large, population-based studies. More modest prospective studies in special population groups, however, may yield useful information at this time. For example, inquiry about whether the pregnancy period is protective against, and the postpartum state conducive to, the development of mental and depressive illness should be extended. It does not seem likely that further retrospective studies will advance this thesis, because of limitations on obtaining adequate psychiatric information. A prospective study, made with special population groups of healthy women of childbearing age who receive routine periodic examinations or are being followed for other purposes, would appear to be worthwhile and timely.

Retrospective studies. Many of the prevailing theories about characteristics and determinants of depression can be tested by retrospective case-control studies in which persons with depressions are compared with nonaffected general population controls. The most serious obstacles to the selection of suitable cases of depression for such studies are poor diagnostic consistency and the lack of representativeness of the cases. In order to overcome these difficulties, it is not sufficient simply to use operational definitions developed and agreed to by experienced and competent psychiatrists, as has been done in some investigations. Such operational definitions need to be applied to representative groups of the affected population, because diagnoses are influenced not only by the preconceived opinions of the examiner but also by the characteristics of the examinee and the setting and circumstances of the examination.

A representative sample of all depressed persons in the community can be drawn from multiple sources: from hospitals, clinics, private psychiatrists, a sample of other physicians, and a probability sample of the general population (screened by a simple questionnaire on depression). The individuals selected in this way can then be regrouped according to the symptom clusters and descriptive syndromes agreed upon by psychiatrists as the operational definitions of the various types of depressive states. The newly constituted diagnostic groups can then be used for comparison with appropriate general population controls to test a number of theories about biologic, psychologic, and social characteristics of depressives.

One of the most interesting observations, and one that has received relatively little attention since it was made by Faris and Dunham, concerns the social and environmental distribution of the major depressive psychosis. Unlike the pattern for schizophrenia and other psychoses, the distribution of manic-depressive psychosis in the community, as judged by first mental hospital admissions, is not materially affected by social status and its numerous correlates or by marital status. These important observations should be extended and tested.

Psychodynamic interpretations of the nature and causes of depressive and other mental disturbances have been almost totally excluded from epidemiologic investigations. Although the difficulties of translating many of the concepts into testable form are evident, it seems regrettable that a greater effort has not been made to do so. The outstanding and constantly described characteristic of most depressive disorders, in Western societies at least, is the important role played by feelings of guilt and self-reproach. The extent to which this characteristic distinguishes depressive subjects from those without depressions needs much investigation.

Epilogue

The relationships among various scientific approaches and bodies of knowledge have been explored not from the viewpoint of multidisciplinary teamwork but as necessary interdependencies. In another context, this view was eloquently expressed by Martin Buber (36): "Certainly, in the course of the history of the spirit each science that has detached itself from a comprehensive context and insured for itself the independence of its realm has just thereby severely and ever more severely limited its subject and the manner of its working. But the investigator cannot truthfully maintain his relationship with reality—a relationship without which all his work becomes a well-regulated game—if he does not again and again, whenever it is necessary, gaze beyond the limits into a sphere which is not his sphere of work, yet which he must contemplate with all his power of research in order to do justice to his own task."

APPENDICES

Table 1.–Depressive Disorders as Classified in the American Psychiatric Association 1952 Manual[a]

Disorders of Psychogenic Origin or without Clearly Defined Physical Cause or Structural Change in the Brain	Code No.[b]
Psychotic Disorders	
Schizophrenic reaction, schizo-affective type	300.6
Involutional psychotic reaction	302
Affective reactions	301.2
Manic-depressive reaction, manic type	301.0
Manic-depressive reaction, depressive type	301.1
Manic-depressive reaction, other	301.2
Psychotic depressive reaction	309.0
Psychoneurotic Disorders	
Depressive reaction	314
Personality Disorders	
Cyclothymic personality	320.2
Supplementary Terms—Diagnostic Terms Used in the Standard Nomenclature of Diseases	
Depression (not otherwise specified)	790.2

[a] Adapted from American Psychiatric Association: *Diagnostic and Statistical Manual Mental Disorders*. Washington, D.C., 1952.
[b] World Health Organization: *International Classification of Diseases,* Vol. 1, 7th Rev., 1955. Geneva: WHO, 1957.

Table 2.–Depressive Disorders as Classified in International Classification of Diseases, 8th Revision, 1965[a]

	Code No.
Psychoses	290–299
Schizophrenia, schizo-affective type	295.7
Affective psychoses	296
Involutional melancholia	296.0
Manic-depressive psychosis, manic type	296.1
Manic-depressive psychosis, depressed type	296.2
Manic-depressive psychosis, circular type	296.3
Other	296.8
Unspecified	296.9
Other psychoses	298
Reactive depressive psychosis	298.0
Neuroses	300
Depressive neurosis	300.4
Personality Disorders	301
Affective (cyclothymic personality)	301.1

[a] World Health Organization: *International Classification of Diseases,* 8th Rev., 1965. Geneva: WHO, 1967.

TABLE 3.—NUMBER AND PERCENT DISTRIBUTION OF FIRST ADMISSIONS AND RESIDENT PATIENTS AT END OF YEAR IN STATE AND COUNTY MENTAL HOSPITALS, BY SELECTED DIAGNOSES, UNITED STATES, 1950, 1955 AND 1963[a]

Diagnosis	First Admissions			Resident Patients		
	1950	1955	1963	1950	1955	1963
	Number					
All Mental Disorders	114,054	122,284	131,997	512,501	558,922	504,604
Brain Syndromes						
Diseases of the Senium	44,113	39,753	32,885	134,849	138,600	116,014
Syphilitic	29,533	29,585	24,493	63,659	73,717	63,398
Other (excl. Alcoholism)	3,862	1,603	318	33,378	29,113	16,117
	10,718	8,565	8,074	37,812	35,770	36,499
Functional Psychoses						
Schizophrenic Reaction	39,269	39,548	35,535	298,248	333,274	298,218
Affective and Involutional	26,559	28,482	26,149	232,044	267,603	253,655
Other	11,496	9,679	8,419	53,323	50,937	36,897
	1,214	1,387	967	12,881	14,734	7,666
Disorders Assoc. with						
Alcoholism	13,767	17,403	20,236	16,404	17,351	21,072
Brain Syndromes	5,105	6,335	6,412	11,151	12,265	15,295
Addiction	8,662	11,068	13,824	5,253	5,086	5,777
Psychoneurosis	5,662	6,549	14,216	5,668	5,415	7,694
Personality Disorders (excl. Alcoholism)	3,393	8,730	18,846	4,530	9,739	13,912
Mental Deficiency	4,149	3,804	3,735	48,190	47,577	42,121
All Other	3,701	6,497	6,544	4,612	6,966	5,573

TABLE 3.—(CONTINUED)

Diagnosis	First Admissions			Resident Patients		
	1950	1955	1963	1950	1955	1963
	Percent					
All Mental Disorders	100.0	100.0	100.0	100.0	100.0	100.0
Brain Syndromes	38.7	32.5	24.9	26.3	24.8	23.0
Diseases of the Senium	25.9	24.2	18.6	12.4	13.2	12.6
Syphilitic	3.4	1.3	0.2	6.5	5.2	3.2
Other (excl. Alcoholism)	9.4	7.0	6.1	7.4	6.4	7.2
Functional Psychoses	34.4	32.3	26.9	58.2	59.6	59.1
Schizophrenic Reaction	23.3	23.3	19.8	45.3	47.9	50.3
Affective and Involutional	10.1	7.9	6.4	10.4	9.1	7.3
Other	1.0	1.1	0.7	2.5	2.6	1.5
Disorders Assoc. with Alcoholism	12.1	14.3	15.3	3.2	3.1	4.2
Brain Syndromes	4.5	5.2	4.9	2.2	2.2	3.0
Addiction	7.6	9.1	10.4	1.0	0.9	1.2
Psychoneurosis	5.0	5.4	10.8	1.1	1.0	1.5
Personality Disorders (excl. Alcoholism)	3.0	7.1	14.3	0.9	1.7	2.8
Mental Deficiency	3.6	3.1	2.8	9.4	8.5	8.3
All Other	3.2	5.3	5.0	0.9	1.3	1.1

[a] Taken verbatim from Kramer, M.: Some Implications of Trends in the Usage of Psychiatric Facilities for Community Mental Health Programs and Related Research. National Institute of Mental Health, U.S. Dept. of Health, Education and Welfare, PHS. Washington, D.C.: Public Health Service Publication No. 1434, 1966.

TABLE 4.–FIRST ADMISSION AND RESIDENT PATIENT AGE ADJUSTED RATES,* BY SELECTED DIAGNOSES, STATE AND COUNTY MENTAL HOSPITALS, UNITED STATES, 1950, 1955 AND 1963[a]

Diagnosis	First Admissions			Resident Patients		
	1950	1955	1963	1950	1955	1963
All Mental Disorders	74.7	75.3	72.2	340.9	344.4	272.7
Brain Syndromes	30.1	24.5	16.8	91.6	85.4	60.2
Diseases of the Senium	20.6	18.2	12.2	44.6	45.4	31.6
Syphilitic	2.6	1.0	0.2	22.2	17.9	8.6
Other (excl. Alcoholism)	6.9	5.3	4.4	24.8	22.1	20.0
Functional Psychoses	24.9	24.4	20.0	197.4	205.4	162.9
Schizophrenic Reaction	16.6	17.5	14.8	152.7	164.9	139.5
Affective and Involutional	7.5	6.0	4.7	35.9	31.4	19.4
Other	0.8	0.9	0.5	8.8	9.1	4.0
Disorders Assoc. with Alcoholism	9.0	10.7	11.5	10.9	10.7	11.5
Brain Syndromes	3.3	3.9	3.6	7.5	7.6	8.2
Addiction	5.7	6.8	7.9	3.4	3.1	3.3
Psychoneurosis	3.6	4.0	8.1	3.7	3.3	4.2
Personality Disorders (excl. Alcoholism)	2.1	5.4	10.2	2.9	6.0	7.5
Mental Deficiency	2.6	2.3	2.0	31.3	29.3	23.4
All Other	2.4	4.0	3.6	3.1	4.3	3.0

* U.S. 1955 civilian population was used as a standard.

[a] Taken verbatim from Kramer, M.: Some Implications of Trends in the Usage of Psychiatric Facilities for Community Mental Health Programs and Related Research. National Institute of Mental Health, U.S. Department of Health, Education, and Welfare, PHS. Washington, D.C.: Public Health Service Publication No. 1434, 1966.

TABLE 5.—FIRST ADMISSION RATES PER 100,000 POPULATION TO PUBLIC AND PRIVATE MENTAL HOSPITALS BY AGE AND SEX, UNITED STATES, 1950 AND 1957, ENGLAND AND WALES, 1952 AND 1956[a]

Age	Manic-Depressive						Involutional					
	England & Wales		United States (Public)		United States (Public & Private)		England & Wales		United States (Public)		United States (Public & Private)	
	Male	Female	Male	Female	Male	Female	Male	Female	Male	Female	Male	Female
	1950 & 1952											
Under 15	0.2	0.5		0.1		0.1						
15–24	5.8	11.1	1.6	2.7	2.4	4.6						
25–34	13.7	23.1	3.0	7.2	5.0	13.5				0.2	0.2	0.1
35–44	20.1	40.7	5.6	9.6	9.2	18.6	0.4	4.9	0.5	5.0	1.2	0.3
45–54	29.5	48.5	6.2	7.5	11.1	15.8	4.0	18.5	6.5	20.6	10.6	9.2
55–64	40.3	49.2	5.4	6.5	9.3	12.7	8.0	12.4	10.6	16.2	16.4	36.9
65+	24.0	25.7	2.4	2.5	4.5	6.1	2.5	3.0	2.5	2.7	5.6	31.5
												7.0
	1956 & 1957											
Under 15	0.2	0.2	0.6	0.9	1.1	1.6						
15–24	8.6	12.1	1.3	2.7	2.2	5.0				0.1	0.2	0.2
25–34	20.6	37.6	2.2	3.5	3.6	6.3	0.3	4.8	0.4	4.0	0.2	0.5
35–44	31.4	51.4	3.2	3.3	5.4	6.8	3.8	21.2	5.5	18.0	0.9	6.3
45–54	41.6	57.5	2.8	3.3	5.3	6.9	8.0	15.7	10.3	16.4	8.5	26.8
55–64	60.3	72.6	1.7	3.4	3.1	4.9	5.5	6.4	4.7	6.1	15.1	26.5
65–74	45.3	57.6	0.3	2.1	1.1	1.8	0.9	1.1	0.5	0.7	7.3	11.1
75+	19.0	21.0		0.7							1.6	2.2

[a] Taken verbatim from a larger table in Kramer, M.: Some Implications of Trends in the Usage of Psychiatric Facilities for Community Mental Health Programs and Related Research. National Institute of Mental Health, U.S. Department of Health, Education, and Welfare, PHS. Washington, D.C.: Public Health Service Publication No. 1434, 1966.

TABLE 6.–CHANGES IN THE SUICIDE RATE IN
PRINCIPAL COUNTRIES OF THE WORLD[a]

Country	Death Rates per 100,000		
	1910–1914	1926–1930	1960
United States (Original Registration States)	15.4	15.0	10.6[1]
England and Wales	9.9	12.3	11.2
Scotland	5.7	9.8	7.8
Irish Free State	3.2	3.3	3.0
Holland	6.2	7.1	6.6
Sweden	17.6	14.5	17.4
Norway	6.0	6.5	6.4
Denmark	18.6	16.8	20.3
Finland	9.6	16.8[2]	20.4
France	22.2	19.1[3]	15.9
Belgium	14.0[4]	15.8	14.6
Germany	21.9	25.9	18.8[5]
Austria	25.7	35.3	23.0
Switzerland	23.7	25.3	19.0
Italy	8.5	9.6	6.3
Spain	5.1[6]	4.7	5.2[7]
Australia	12.8	12.2	10.6
New Zealand	12.1	13.9	9.7
South Africa	10.5[8]	11.2[2]	12.2[7]
Japan	19.0	20.6	21.3

[1] Total United States
[2] 1926–1929
[3] 1926–1928
[4] 1910–1913
[5] West Germany
[6] 1911–1914
[7] 1959
[8] 1912–1914

[a] Taken verbatim from: Dublin, L. I.: *Suicide* (New York: The Ronald Press Company, 1963, p. 211). 1960 rates from United Nations, *Demographic Yearbook, 1961*, World Health Organization, *Epidemiological and Vital Statistics Report*, Vol. 14, No. 5 (1961).

TABLE 7.–DEPRESSION AND SUICIDE:
RATES PER 100,000 (REGISTRAR-GENERAL, 1959, 1960)[a]

	Depression*		Suicide	
Age	Male	Female	Male	Female
45 –	55	90	22	16
55 –	80	101	35	20
65 –	57	72	43	22
75 +	24	25	49	14

* First admissions in 1956 of endogenous, reactive and involutional depressions.

[a] Taken verbatim from Sainsbury, P.: Suicide in Later Life. *Geront. Clin.* 4:161–70, 1962.

TABLE 8.—DEATH BY SUICIDE IN MANIC-DEPRESSIVE DISEASE:
A SUMMARY OF FIVE FOLLOW-UP STUDIES[a]

Investigator	No. Cases	No. Dead	Percent Dead	No. Dead by Suicide	Percent Dead by Suicide	Percent of Deaths Due to Suicide
Langelüddecke*	341	268	78.8	41	12.0	15.3
Slater	138	59	42.8	9	6.5	15.3
Lundquist	319	119	37.4	17	5.3	14.3
Schulz*	2004	492	24.5	66	3.3	13.4
Stenstedt	216	42	19.4	6	14.3	
Mean‡						14.5†

* Original article not consulted, reviewed in Stenstedt.
† The figure of 14.5 per cent in the text is this mean. Since there is so little variation in the proportion of deaths by suicide despite the great variation in the proportion who died from any cause, it is assumed that had all patients been followed until their deaths the proportion dead by suicide would have remained near 14.5 per cent.
‡ Not weighted for the differing numbers of cases.

[a] Taken verbatim from Robins, E., Murphy, G. E., Wilkinson, R. H., Gassner, S. and Kayes, J.: Some Clinical Considerations in the Prevention of Suicide Based on a Study of 134 Successful Suicides. *Amer. J. Pub. Health*, 49:888–99, 1959.

TABLE 9.–RATES OF FIRST ADMISSIONS TO HOSPITALS FOR THE INSANE, CLASSIFIED BY DIAGNOSIS AND NATIVITY[a]

	Material of Odegaard's study		Malzberg's New York Material		
	Norwegian-born of Minnesota	Norwegians of Norway	Foreign-born	Native-born	Native-born of native parentage
Schizophrenia	100	50	100	68	51
Manic-depressive psychosis	100	110	100	79	70
General paresis	100	73	100	98	78
Alcoholic psychosis	100	34	100	94	69
Senile psychosis	100	13	100	75	55
Arteriosclerosis			100	81	65

[a] Adapted from: Ödegaard, O.: Emigration and Mental Health. *Ment. Hyg.*, 19:635-660, October, 1935.

TABLE 10.–FIRST ADMISSION RATES BY SOCIAL CLASS PER 100,000 MALES AGES 20 AND OVER, ENGLAND AND WALES, 1956[a]

Diagnosis	Social Class				
	I	II	III	IV	V
All diagnoses	103	89	106	105	205
Schizophrenia	11	8	16	17	45
Manic-depressive Reaction	32	26	31	29	52

[a] From Brooke, E. M.: National Statistics in the Epidemiology of Mental Illness. *J. Ment. Sci.* 105:893-908, 1959.

TABLE 11.—Percentage Distribution of Manic-Depressive and Schizophrenic Psychoses by Sex, According to Marital Condition, with Comparable Data from the Chicago Population in 1930[a]

Marital Condition	Manic-Depressive Psychoses							Schizophrenia							Population 1930		
	Male		Female		Total		Male		Female		Total		Male %	Female %	Total %
	No.	%	No.	%	No.	%	No.	%	No.	%	No.	%			
Single	246	29.3	305	20.7	551	23.8	3,621	66.6	1,732	33.7	5,353	50.6	36.5	27.9	32.3
Married	377	44.9	645	43.9	1,022	44.2	1,073	19.7	2,218	43.2	3,291	31.1	58.0	59.2	58.6
Widowed	30	3.6	93	6.3	123	5.3	95	1.7	268	5.2	363	3.4	4.0	11.0	7.4
Divorced	24	2.7	30	2.0	54	2.4	128	2.4	174	3.4	302	2.9	1.3	1.8	1.6
Unknown	168	19.3	399	27.1	561	24.3	518	9.6	748	14.5	1,266	12.0	0.2	0.1	0.1
Total	839	100.0	1,472	100.0	2,311	100.0	5,435	100.0	5,140	100.0	10,575	100.0	100.0	100.0	100.0

[a] Adapted from two appendix tables in Faris, R. E. L. and Dunham, H. W.; Mental Disorders in Urban Areas: An Ecological Study of Schizophrenia and Other Psychoses, Chicago, Ill.: Univ. of Chicago Press, 1939, pp. 241–42.

TABLE 12.—HETEROGENEOUS TWIN SIBSHIP DATA ON THE EXPECTED INCIDENCE OF MANIC-DEPRESSIVE PSYCHOSIS[a]

	Number of Cases			Partly Uncorrected Morbidity Rates			
	Siblings (Half-Sibs)	Dizygotic Twin Pairs	Monozygotic Twin Pairs	Half-Sibs	Siblings	Dizygotic Co-Twins	Monozygotic Co-Twins
Rosanoff et al.	?	67	23		1.5	16.4	69.6
Luxenburger et al.	263	13(3)*	4(29)*		12.7	0.0-33.3*	75.0-96.6*
Schulz (Ruedin)	844 (124)			1.4	7.4-23.8 11.7		
Slater	171	30	6			23.3	66.7
Kallmann	206 (16)	55	27	12.5	18.0	23.6	92.6

* Casuistically reported cases.

[a] Taken verbatim from Kallmann, F. J.: Genetic Principles in Manic-Depressive Psychosis. In *Depression*, ed. P. H. Hoch and J. Zubin, p. 5. New York: Grune and Stratton, 1954.

TABLE 13.–TUBERCULOSIS IN 308 TWIN INDEX-FAMILIES[a]

Relationship to Twin Index	Number Observed	Tuberculosis Cases	Percentage
General population (Estimate—New York State)			1.1
Spouse	226	14	6.2
Half-sibling	42	4	9.5
Parent	688	114	16.6
Sibling	720	136	18.9
Dizygotic co-twin	230	42	18.3
Monozygotic co-twin	78	48	61.5

[a] Adapted from a table in Kallmann, F. J. and Reisner, D.: Twin Studies on the Significance of Genetic Factors in Tuberculosis. Amer. Rev. Tuberc., 47:549–74, 1943.

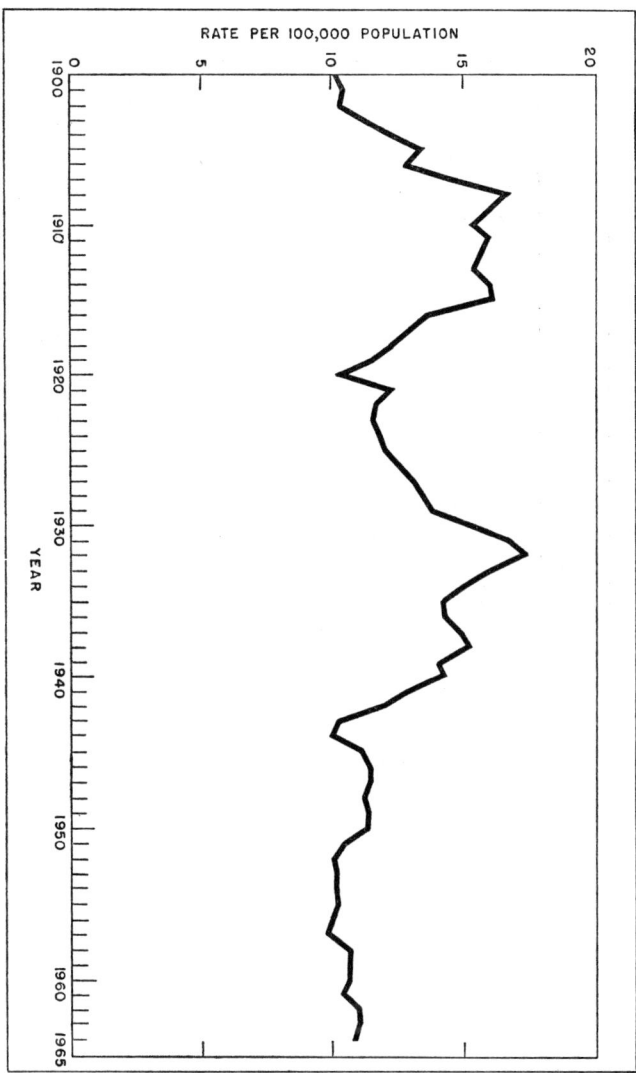

FIGURE 1.–SUICIDE RATES: DEATH REGISTRATION STATES, 1900-1932, AND UNITED STATES, 1933-1964. FROM: U. S. DEPARTMENT OF HEALTH, EDUCATION, AND WELFARE, PUBLIC HEALTH SERVICE, NATIONAL CENTER FOR HEALTH STATISTICS. SUICIDE IN THE UNITED STATES 1950-1964. PHS PUBLICATION NO. 1000, SERIES 20, NO. 5, AUGUST 1967.

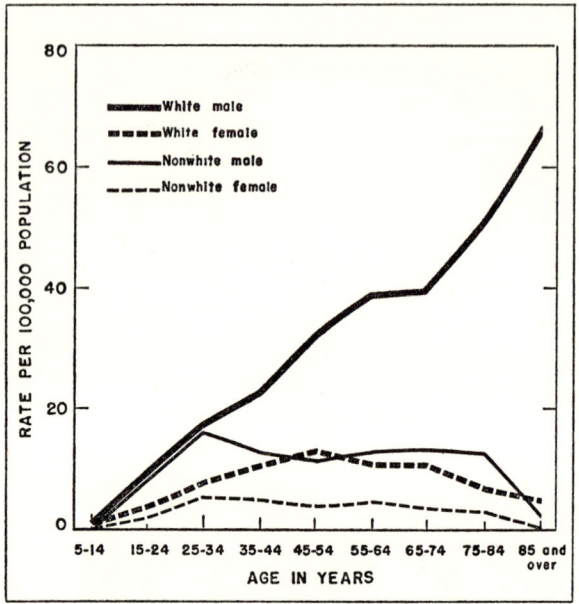

FIGURE 2.–SUICIDE RATES BY COLOR, SEX AND AGE: 1964. FROM: U. S. DEPARTMENT OF HEALTH, EDUCATION, AND WELFARE, PUBLIC HEALTH SERVICE, NATIONAL CENTER FOR HEALTH STATISTICS. SUICIDE IN THE UNITED STATES 1950-1964. PHS PUBLICATION NO. 1000, SERIES 20, NO. 5, AUGUST 1967.

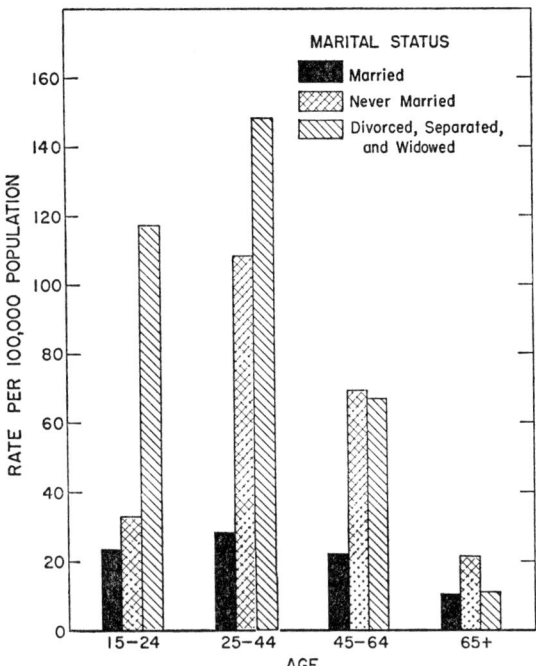

*For MRA Cohort Study
Arkansas, California, Illinois, Kentucky, Louisiana, Michigan, Minnesota, New York, North Carolina, Ohio, Pennsylvania, Tennessee, Wisconsin

FIGURE 3.–FIRST ADMISSION RATES OF PATIENTS WITH FUNCTIONAL PSYCHOTIC DISORDERS, STATE AND COUNTY MENTAL HOSPITALS, BY MARITAL STATUS AND AGE, MRA COHORT STUDY, 1960. FROM: KRAMER, M.: SOME IMPLICATIONS OF TRENDS IN THE USAGE OF PSYCHIATRIC FACILITIES FOR COMMUNITY MENTAL HEALTH PROGRAMS AND RELATED RESEARCH. NATIONAL INSTITUTE OF MENTAL HEALTH, U. S. DEPARTMENT OF HEALTH, EDUCATION, AND WELFARE, PUBLIC HEALTH SERVICE. PHS PUBLICATION NO. 1434, 1966.

SELECTED BIBLIOGRAPHY

1. Abraham, K.: *Selected Papers on Psychoanalysis.* New York: Basic Books, 1953.
2. Abramson, J. H.: The Cornell Medical Index as an Epidemiological Tool. *Amer. J. Public Health* 56:287–96, February 1966.
3. Ackerknecht, E. H.: Psychopathology, Primitive Medicine and Primitive Culture. *Bull. Hist. Med.* 14:30–67, June 1943,
4. Acheson, E. D.: The Clinical Syndrome Variously Called Benign Myalgic Encephalomyelitis or Iceland Disease and Epidemic Neuromyasthenia. *Amer. J. Med.* 26:569–95, April 1959.
5. Allen, G., and Redekop, C.: Individual Differences in Survival and Reproduction Among Old Colony Mennonites in Mexico: Progress to October 1966. *Eugenics Quart.* 14:103–11, June 1967.
6. American Psychiatric Association: *Diagnostic and Statistical Manual: Mental Disorders.* Washington, D.C.: American Psychiatric Association, 1952.
7. American Public Health Association, Program Area Committee on Mental Health: *Mental Disorders: A Guide to Control Methods.* New York: APHA, 1962.

8. Arieti, S.: Manic-Depressive Psychosis. In *American Handbook of Psychiatry*, ed. S. Arieti, 1:419–54. New York: Basic Books, 1959.
9. Astrup, C., and Ödegaard, O.: Internal Migration and Mental Disease in Norway. *Psychiat. Quart.* Suppl. 34:116, 1960.
10. Asuni, T.: Suicide in Western Nigeria. *Brit. Med. J.* 2:1091–97, Oct. 27, 1962.
11. Ayd, F. J.: Suicide: A Hazard in Depression. *J. Neuropsychiat.* 2:S52–54, February 1961.
12. Baastrup, P. C., and Schou, M.: Lithium as a Prophylactic Agent. *Arch. Gen. Psychiat.* 16 (2):162–72, 1967.
13. Babigian, H. M., Gardner, E. A., Miles, H. C., and Romano, J.: Diagnostic Consistency in a Follow-up Study of 1215 Patients. *Amer. J. Psychiat.* 121:895–901, March 1965.
14. Bahn, A. K., Chandler, C. A., and Lemkau, P. V.: Diagnostic Characteristics of Adult Out-patients of Psychiatric Clinics as Related to Type and Outcome of Services. *Milbank Mem. Fund Quart.* 15:407–42, October 1962.
15. Bahn, A. K., Gardner, E. A., Alltop, L. Knatterud, G. L., and Solomon, M.: Admission and Prevalence Rates for Psychiatric Facilities in Four Register Areas. *Amer. J. Public Health* 56:2033–51, December 1966.
16. Bakwin, H.: Pseudodoxia Pediatrica. *New Eng. J. Med.* 232:691–97, June 14, 1945.
17. Batchelor, I. R. C., and Napier, M. B.: Attempted Suicides in Old Age. *Brit. Med. J.* 2:1186–90, 1953.
18. Beck, A. T.: *Depression: Clinical, Experimental and Theoretical Aspects.* New York: Harper & Row, 1967.
19. Beck, A. T., Ward, C. H., Mendelson, M., Mock, J., and Erbaugh, J.: Reliability of Psychiatric Diagnoses: 1. A Critique of Systematic Studies. *Amer. J. Psychiat.* 119:210–16, September 1962.
20. Beck, A. T., Ward, C. H., Mendelson, M., Mock, J., and Erbaugh, J.: Reliability of Psychiatric Diagnoses: 2. A Study of Consistency of Clinical Judgments and Ratings. *Amer. J. Psychiat.* 119:351–57, October 1962.
21. Bellak, L. (with Pasquarelli, B., Parkes, E., and Bellak, S. S.): *Manic-Depressive Psychosis and Allied Conditions.* New York: Grune & Stratton, 1952.
22. Bender, L.: *Psychopathic Behavior Disorders in Children, Handbook of Correctional Psychology,* p. 360. New York: Philosophical Library, 1947.

SELECTED BIBLIOGRAPHY

23. Bibring, E.: The Mechanism of Depression. In *Affective Disorders*, ed. P. Greenacre. New York: International Universities Press, 1953.
24. Bigelow, N: The Involutional Psychoses. In *An American Handbook of Psychiatry*, ed. S. Arieti, Vol. 1. New York: Basic Books, 1959.
25. Bille, M., and Juel-Nielsen, N.: Incidence of Neurosis in Psychiatric and Other Medical Services in a Danish County. *Danish Med. Bull.* 10:172–76, 1963.
26. Birkelo, C. C., Chamberlain, W. E., Phelps, P.S., Schools, P.E., Zacks, D., and Yerushalmy, J.: Tuberculosis Case Finding. *J. A. M. A.* 133:359–65, February 8, 1947.
27. Bleuler, E.: *Textbook of Psychiatry*. New York: The Macmillan Co., 1924.
28. Blum, R. H.: Case Identification in Psychiatric Epidemiology: Methods and Problems. *Milbank Mem. Fund Quart.* 40:253–85, July 1962.
29. Bodian, C., Gardner, E. A., Willis, E. M., and Bahn, A. K.: Socioeconomic Indicators from Census Tract Data Related to Rates of Mental Illness. In Papers Presented at the Census Tract Conference, September 5, 1963. Washington, D.C.: U.S. Dept. of Commerce, Bureau of the Census.
30. Böök, J. A.: A Genetic and Neuropsychiatric Investigation of a North Swedish Population with Special Regard to Schizophrenia and Mental Deficiency. *Acta Genet. Stat. Med.* 4:1–100, 1953.
31. Bowlby, J.: Childhood Mourning and Its Implications for Psychiatry. *Amer. J. Psychiat.* 118:481–98, 1961.
32. Bragg, R. L. Risk of Admission to Mental Hospital Following Hysterectomy or Cholecystectomy. *Amer. J. Public Health* 55:1403–10, September 1965.
33. Brooke, E. M.: A Cohort Study of Patients First Admitted to Mental Hospitals in 1954 and 1955, *General Register Office Studies on Medical and Population Subjects No. 18*. London: Her Majesty's Stationery Office, 1963.
34. Brown, F.: Depression and Childhood Bereavement. *J. Ment. Sci.*, 107:754–77, 1961.
35. Brown, F.: Childhood Bereavement and Subsequent Psychiatric Disorder. *Brit. J. Psychiat.* 112:1035–41, 1966.
36. Buber, M: Guilt and Guilt Feelings (trans. R.G. Smith), The William Alanson White Memorial Lectures, Fourth Series. *Psychiatry* 20:114–29, May 1957.

37. Bunney, W. E., Jr., Davis, J. M., Weil-Malherbe, H., and Smith, E. R. B.: Biochemical Changes in Psychotic Depression. *Arch. Gen. Psychiat.* 16:448–60, April 1967.
38. Bunney, W. E., Jr., Hartmann, E. L.: Study of a Patient with 48-hour Manic-Depressive Cycles. I. An Analysis of Behavioral Factors. II. (with J. W. Mason) Strong Positive Correlation Between Endocrine Factors and Manic Defense Patterns. *Arch. Gen. Psychiat.* 12:611–18, 619–25, 1965.
39. Bunney, W. E., Jr., Mason, J. W., Roatch, J. F., and Hamburg, D. A.: A Psychoendocrine Study of Severe Psychotic Depressive Crises. *Amer. J. Psychiat.*, 122:72–80, July 1965.
40. Cade, J. F. J.: Lithium Salts in the Treatment of Psychotic Excitement. *Med. J. Australia* 2:349–53, September 3, 1949.
41. Cameron, N.: The Place of Mania Among the Depressions from a Biological Standpoint. *J. Psychol.* 14:181–95, 1942.
42. Carstairs G. M. Characteristics of the Suicide Prone. *Proc. Royal Soc. Med.* 54:262–64, 1961.
43. Carstairs, G. M.: In *Transcultural Psychiatry,* ed. A. V. S. deRueck and R. Porter, p. 364. Boston: Little, Brown & Co., 1965.
44. Cassel, J.: Social Science Theory as a Source of Hypotheses in Epidemiological Research. *Amer. J. Public Health,* 54:1482–88, September 1964.
45. Caudill, W., and Doi, L. T.: Psychiatry and Culture in Japan. In *Man's Image in Medicine and Anthropology,* ed. I. Galdston. New York: International Universities Press, Inc., 1963.
46. Cavan, R. S.: *Suicide.* Chicago: University of Chicago Press, 1928.
47. Clark, R. E.: Psychoses, Income and Occupational Prestige. *Amer. J. Sociol.* 54:433–40, March 1949.
48. Clausen, J. A.: Values, Norms and the Health Called "Mental": Purpose and Feasibility of Assessment. Presented at a Symposium on Definition and Measurement of Mental Health, National Center for Health Statistics, U. S. Public Health Service, Washington, D.C. 1966-67.
49. Clausen, J. A., and Kohn, M. L.: Relation of Schizophrenia to the Social Structure of a Small City. In: Pasamanick, B., ed.: *Epidemiology of Mental Disorder.* Washington, D.C.: Publication No. 60, American Association for Advancement of Science, 1959.
50. Clayton, P. J., Pitts, F. N. and Winokur, G.: Affective Disorder IV, Mania. *Compr. Psychiat.* 6:313, 1965.

51. Cohen, M. B., Baker, G., Cohen, R. A., Fromm-Reichmann, F., and Weigert, E. V.: An Intensive Study of Twelve Cases of Manic-Depressive Psychosis. *Psychiatry* 17:103–37, May 1954.
52. Cohen, B. M., and Fairbank, R. E.: Statistical Contributions from the Mental Hygiene Study of the Eastern Health District of Baltimore. *Amer. J. Psychiat.* 94:1153–61, March 1938.
53. Cohen, B. M., and Fairbank, R. E.: Statistical Contributions from the Mental Hygiene Study of the Eastern Health District of Baltimore. *Amer. J. Psychiat.* 94:1377–95, May 1938.
54. Cole, J. O.: Therapeutic Efficacy of Antidepressant Drugs: A Review. *J. A. M. A.* 1940. 190:448, November 2, 1964.
55. Cole, J. O.: The Drug Approach to Mental Illness. 126th Lowell Lecture, Tufts University School of Medicine, Boston, Mass., Jan. 30, 1967.
56. Cooper, B.: Psychiatric Disorder in Hospital and General Practice. *Social Psychiat.* 1:7–10, August 1966.
57. Cooper, J. E.: Diagnostic Change in a Longitudinal Study of Psychiatric Patients. *Brit. J. Psychiat.* 113:129–42, 1967.
58. Coppen, A.: Biochemical Aspects of Affective Disorders. Sixth World Congress of Psychiatry, Madrid, Spain, September 5–11, 1966. *Abstracts, International Congress Series No. 117,* p. 25. Amsterdam: Excerpta Medica Foundation, 1966.
59. Coppen, A., Shaw, D. M., and Mangoni, A.: Total Exchangeable Sodium in Depressive Illness, *Brit. Med. J.* 295, 1962.
60. Cowie, V., and Slater, E.: Psychiatric Genetics. In: *Recent Progress in Psychiatry*, Vol. 3 ed. G. W. T. H. Fleming and A. Walk, pp. 1–53. New York: Grove Press, Inc., 1959.
61. Cutler, R. P., and Kurland, H. D.: Clinical Quantification of Depressive Reactions. *Arch. Gen. Psychiat.* 5:280–85, 1961.
62. Dalgard, O. S.: Migration and Functional Psychoses in Oslo. Sixth World Congress of Psychiatry, Madrid, Spain, September 5–11, 1966. *Abstracts, International Congress Series No. 117,* p. 156. Amsterdam: Excerpta Medica Foundation, 1966.
63. Dalton, K.: Menstruation and Acute Psychiatric Illnesses. *Brit. Med. J.* 1:148–49, 1959.
64. Davies, E. B., ed.: *Depression.* Proceedings of the Symposium held at Cambridge September 22–26, 1959. Cambridge: Cambridge University Press, 1964.
65. Dayton, N. A.: *New Facts on Mental Disorders.* Springfield, Ill.: Chas. C Thomas, 1940.
66. Dennehy, C. M.: Childhood Bereavement and Psychiatric Illness. *Brit. J. Psychiat.* 112:1049–69, 1966.

67. *Depression and Suicide in Adolescents and Young Adults.* Proceedings of a Conference at Bonnie Oaks Lodge, Fairlee, Vermont, June 6–8, 1966. A Technical Assistance Project sponsored by three Northern New England States and the National Institute of Mental Health.
68. Diethelm, O.: The Fallacy of the Concept: Psychosis. In *Current Problems in Psychiatric Diagnosis*, ed. P. H. Hoch and J. Zubin, pp. 24–32. New York: Grune & Stratton, 1953.
69. Dohrenwend, B. P., and Dohrenwend, B. S.: The Problem of Validity in Field Studies of Psychological Disorder. *J. Abnorm. Psychol.* 70:52–69, February 1965.
70. Dorn, H. F.: Some Problems for Research in Mortality and Morbidity. Public Health Rep. 71:1–5, January, 1956.
71. Downes, J., and Simon, K.: Characteristics of Psychoneurotic Patients and Their Families as Revealed in a General Morbidity Study. *Psychosom. Med.* 15:463–75, September-October 1953.
72. Dublin, L. I.: *Suicide: A Sociological and Statistical Study.* New York: The Ronald Press Co., 1963.
73. Dublin, L. I., and Bunzel, B.: *To Be or Not to Be.* New York: Harrison Smith and Robert Haas, 1933.
74. Du Bois, F. S.: Rhythms, Cycles and Periods in Health and Disease. *Amer. J. Psychiat.* 116:114–19, 1959.
75. Dubos, R., and Dubos, J.: *The White Plague.* Boston: Little, Brown & Co., 1952.
76. Dubos, R., Savage, D., and Schaedler, R.: Biological Freudianism: Lasting Effects of Early Environmental Influences. *Pediatrics,* 38:789–800, November 1966.
77. Dunham, H. W.: *Community and Schizophrenia. An Epidemiological Analysis.* Lafayette Clinic Monographs in Psychiatry. Detroit: Wayne State University Press, 1965.
78. Durkheim, E.: *Le Suicide* (Paris: Librairie Felix Alcan, 1912), trans. J. A. Spaulding, J. A. and G. Simpson. New York: Free Press, 1951.
79. Duval, H. J., Locke, B. Z., and Kramer, M.: Psychoneuroses Among the First Admissions to Psychiatric Facilities in Ohio: 1958–1961. *Community Mental Health* 2:237–43, 1966.
80. Eaton, J. W., and Weil, R. J.: *Culture and Mental Disorders: A Comparative Study of the Hutterites and Other Populations.* New York: Free Press, 1955.

SELECTED BIBLIOGRAPHY

81. Elkind, H. B., Zubin, J., and Myerson, A.: Are Mental Diseases on the Increase? *Psychiat. Quart.* 13:165–81, 1938.
82. Engel, G. L., and Reichsman, F.: Spontaneous and Experimentally Induced Depressions in an Infant with a Gastric Fistula. *J. Amer. Psychoanalyt. Ass.* 4:428, 1956.
83. Engel, G. L., Reichsman, F., and Segal, H. L.: A Study of an Infant with a Gastric Fistula. *Psychosom. Med.* 18:374–98, 1956.
84. Esquirol, J. E. D.: *Mental Maladies; a Treatise on Insanity.* New York: Hafner Publishing Co., Inc. 1965.
85. Essen-Möller, E.: A Current Field Study in the Mental Disorders in Sweden. In *Comparative Epidemiology of the Mental Disorders.* Ed. P. H. Hoch and J. Zubin. New York: Grune & Stratton, 1961.
86. Essen-Möller, E.: Individual Traits and Morbidity in a Swedish Rural Population. *Acta Psychiat. Neurol. Scand.* Suppl. 100:1–160, 1956.
87. Essen-Möller, E., and Hagnell, O.: The Frequency and Risk of Depression Within a Rural Population in Scania. *Acta Psychiat. Scand.* Suppl. 162, 37:28, 1961.
88. Ettlinger, R., and Flordh, P.: Attempted Suicide. *Acta Psychiat. Neurolog. Scand. Suppl.* 103:1–45, 1955.
89. Ewald, G.: Psychoses in Acute Infections. *Handbook of Mental Diseases,* Vol. 7, ed. Bumke, pp. 314, 330. Berlin: Springer, 1928.
90. Farberow, N. L., and Shneidman, E. S.: *The Cry for Help.* New York: McGraw-Hill, 1961.
91. Faris, R. E. L., and Dunham, H. W.: *Mental Disorders in Urban Areas: An Ecological Study of Schizophrenia and Other Psychoses.* Chicago: University of Chicago Press, 1939.
92. Foulds, G. A.: *Personality and Personal Illness.* Philadelphia: J. B. Lippincott Co., 1965.
93. Frank, R.: *The Organized Adaptive Aspects of the Depression-Elation Response.* In *Depression,* ed. P. H. Hoch and J. Zubin. New York: Grune & Stratton, 1954.
94. Freud, A.: *Normality and Pathology in Childhood.* New York: International Universities Press, Inc., 1965.
95. Freud, S.: Mourning and Melancholia. In: *Collected Papers IV.* London: Hogarth Press, 1925.
96. Friedman, S. A., Cowitz, B., Cohen, H. W. and Granick, S.: Syndromes and Themes of Psychotic Depression. *Arch. Gen. Psychiat.* 9:504–09, 1963.

97. Frumkin, R. M.: Some Social Factors in Involutional Psychosis. *Ohio Med. J.* 50:243–44, 1954.
98. Gardner, E. A.: The Role of the Classification System in Outpatient Psychiatry. Presented at Conference on the Role and Methodology of Classification in Psychiatry and Psychopathology, American Psychiatric Association, Washington, D.C., November 19–21, 1965.
99. Gardner, E. A., Bahn, A. K., and Mack, M.: Suicide and Psychiatric Care in the Aging. *Arch. Gen. Psychiat.* 10:547–53, 1964.
100. Gardner, E. A., Bahn, A. K., and Miles, H. C.: Patient Experience in Psychiatric Units of General and State Mental Hospitals. *Public Health Rep.* 79:755–67, 1964.
101. Gardner, W. I.: Occurrence of Severe Depressive Reactions in the Mentally Retarded. *Amer. J. Psychiat.* 124:386–90, September 1967.
102. Gero, G.: An Equivalent of Depression: Anorexia. In *Affective Disorders,* ed. P. Greenacre. New York: International Universities Press, 1953.
103. Goldberger, J.: *Pellagra: Its Nature and Prevention.* Washington, D.C.: U.S. Govt. Printing Office, 1927.
104. Goldfarb, A., Moses, L. E., and Downing, J. J.: Reliability of Psychiatrists' Community Case Findings. *Amer. J. Public Health* 57:94–106, January 1967.
105. Goldhamer, H., and Marshall, A.: *Psychosis and Civilization. Two Studies in the Frequency of Mental Disease.* Glencoe, Ill.: Free Press, 1953.
106. Gordon, J. E., Lindemann, E., Ipsen, J., and Vaughan, W. T.: An Epidemiologic Analysis of Suicide. In: *Epidemiology of Mental Disorder* (in Proceedings Annual Conference, Parts 1–3). New York: Milbank Memorial Fund, 1949, pp. 137–75.
107. Gorwitz, K.: A Critique of Past and Present Mental Health Statistics in the United States and a Blueprint for Future Program Development. Submitted as a doctoral thesis, Johns Hopkins University School of Hygiene and Public Health, October 1966.
108. Gottesman, I. I.: Heritability of Personality: A Demonstration. *Psycholog. Monogr.*, General and Applied, 77; whole no. 572, 1963.
109. Gottschalk, L. A.: Depressions—Psychodynamic Considerations. In *Pharmacotherapy of Depression,* ed. J. O. Cole and J. R. Wittenborn. Springfield, Ill.: Chas. C Thomas, 1966.

SELECTED BIBLIOGRAPHY

110. Grad, J. C., and Sainsbury, P.: Mental Illness and the Family. *Lancet,* 1: pp. 544–47, March 9, 1963.
111. Greenacre, P., ed.: *Affective Disorders.* New York: International Universities Press, Inc., 1953.
112. Greenblatt, M., Grosser, G. H., and Wechsler, H.: A Comparative Study of Selected Antidepressant Medication and EST. *Amer. J. Psychiat.* 119:144–53, 1962.
113. Gregory, I.: Studies of Parental Deprivation in Psychiatric Patients. *Amer. J. Psychiat.* 115:432, 1958.
114. Gregory, I.: *Psychiatry: Biological and Social.* Philadelphia: W. B. Saunders Co., 1961.
115. Gregory, I.: Retrospective Data Concerning Childhood Loss of a Parent: II. Category of Parental Loss by Decade of Birth, Diagnosis and MMPI. *Arch. Gen. Psychiat.* 15:362–67, 1966.
116. Grinker, R., Miller, J., Sabshin, M., Nunn, R., and Nunnally, J. C.: *The Phenomena of Depressions.* New York: Paul B. Hoeber, 1961.
117. Group for the Advancement of Psychiatry, Committee on Preventive Psychiatry. Problems of Estimating Changes in Frequency of Mental Disorders. Report No. 50, August 1961.
118. Group for the Advancement of Psychiatry, Committee on Research. Psychiatric Research and the Assessment of Change. Vol. 6, Report No. 63, November 1966.
119. Gruenberg, E.: A Review of Mental Health in the Metropolis, The Midtown Manhattan Study. *Milbank Mem. Fund Quart.* 41:76–94, January 1963.
120. Gruenberg, E.: On Measuring Mental Morbidity. Presented at a Symposium on Definition and Measurement of Mental Health, National Center for Health Statistics, U.S. Public Health Service, Washington, D.C. 1966–67.
121. Hagnell, O.: *A Prospective Study of the Incidence of Mental Disorder.* Lund: Svenska Bokförlaget Norstedts, 1966.
122. Hamilton, J. A.: Postpartum Psychiatric Problems. St. Louis: C. V. Mosby, 1962.
123. Hamilton, M.: A Rating Scale for Depression. *J. Neurol. Neurosurg. Psychiat.* 23:56–62, 1960.
124. Hamilton, M. and White, J. M.: Clinical Syndromes in Depressive States. *J. Ment. Sci.* 105:985–98, 1959.
125. Hammer, M., and Leacock, E.: Source Material on the Epidemiology of Mental Illness. In *Field Studies in the Mental*

Disorders. ed. J. Zubin. pp. 418–86. New York: Grune & Stratton, 1961.
126. Hare, E. H.: Family Setting and the Urban Distribution of Schizophrenia. *J. Ment. Sci.* 102:349, 1956.
127. Hare, E. H.: Mental Illness and Social Conditions in Bristol. *J. Ment. Sci.* 102:349–57, April 1956.
128. Harrow, M., Colbert, J., Detre, T., and Bakeman, R.: Symptomatology and Subjective Experiences in Current Depressive States. *Arch. Gen. Psychiat.* 14:203–12, February 1966.
129. Hathaway, S. R., and McKinley, J. C.: A Multiphasic Personality Schedule (Minnesota): III. The Measurement of Symptomatic Depression. *J. Psychol.* 14:73–84, 1942.
130. Helgason, T.: The Frequency of Depressive States in Iceland as Compared With the Other Scandinavian Countries. *Acta Psychiat. Scand.* Suppl. 162, 37:81–90, 1961.
131. Hill, A. B.: *Principles of Medical Statistics.* New York: Oxford University Press, 1955.
132. Hill, O. W., and Price, J. S.: Childhood Bereavement and Adult Depression. *Brit. J. Psychiat.* 113:743–51, July 1967.
133. Hoch, P. H., and Zubin, J., eds.: *Relation of Psychological Tests to Psychiatry.* New York: Grune & Stratton, 1952.
134. Hoch, P. H., and Zubin, J., eds.: *Current Problems in Psychiatric Diagnosis,* pp. 46–50. New York: Grune & Stratton, 1953.
135. Hoffer, W.: Psychoanalytic Comments on the Psychology and Psychotherapy of Depression. In *Depression,* ed. B. Davies. Cambridge: Cambridge University Press, 1964.
136. Hollingshead, A. B., and Redlich, F. C.: *Social Class and Mental Illness: A Community Study.* New York: John Wiley & Sons, Inc., 1958.
137. Hughes, C., Tremblay, M., Rapaport, R., and Leighton, A. H.: *People of Cove and Woodlot.* The Stirling County Study, Vol. 2. New York: Basic Books, 1960.
138. Hunt, S. M., Jr., Singer, K., and Cobb, S.: The Components of Depression Identified from a Self-rating Depression Inventory for Survey Use. *Arch. Gen. Psychiat.* 16:441–47, April 1967.
139. Hunt, W. A., Arnhoff, F. N., and Cotton, J. W.: Reliability, Chance and Fantasy in Inter-Judge Agreement Among Clinicians. *J. Clin. Psychol.* 10:294, 1954.
140. Hunt, W. A., Wittson, C. L., and Hunt, E. G.: A Theoretical and Practical Analysis of the Diagnostic Process. In *Current*

Problems in Psychiatric Diagnosis, ed. P. H. Hoch and J. Zubin. New York: Grune & Stratton, 1953.
141. Hurst, L. A.: Converging Advances in Psychiatric Genetics and the Pharmacology of Psychotropic Drugs: Research Implications, Medical Proceedings. *Mediese Bydraes,* 7:417–23, October 7, 1961.
142. *International Conference on Medical Psychotherapy,* Vol. III. Based on International Congress on Mental Health, London, 1948. New York: Columbia University Press, 1948.
143. Ivanys, E., Dzdkova, S., and Vana, J.: Prevalence of Psychoses Recorded Among Psychiatric Patients in a Part of the Urban Population. *Cesko. Psychiat.* 60:152–63, 1964.
144. Jaco, E. G.: *The Social Epidemiology of Mental Disorders: A Psychiatric Survey of Texas.* New York: Russell Sage Foundation, 1960.
145. Jacobs, J., and Teicher, J. D.: Broken Homes and Social Isolation in Attempted Suicides of Adolescents. *Int. J. Soc. Psychiat.* 13:139–49, 1967.
146. James, W.: *The Varieties of Religious Experience: A Study in Human Nature.* New York: Longmans, Green and Co., 1923. (Original—Gifford Lectures, Edinburgh University, 1902.)
147. Jeliffe, S. E.: *Some Historical Phases of the Manic-Depressive Psychosis,* Vol. XI. Baltimore: Williams & Wilkins Co., 1931.
148. Jenner, F. A., Gjessing, L. R., Cox, J. R., Davies-Jones, A., Hullin, R. P., and Hanna, S. M.: A Manic-Depressive Psychotic with a Persistent Forty-eight Hour Cycle. *Brit. J. Psychiat.* 501:895–910 August 1967.
149. Jones, D. A. and Miles, H. L.: The Anglesey Mental Health Survey. In *Problems in Medical Care,* ed. G. McLachlen. London: Oxford University Press, 1964.
150. Juel-Nielsen, N., Bille, M., Flygenring, J., and Helgason, T.: Frequency of Depressive States within Geographically Delimited Population Groups. 3. Incidence (The Aarhus County Investigation). *Acta Psychiat. Scand.* Suppl. 162, 37:69–80, 1961.
151. Juel-Nielsen, N., and Strömgren, E.: Five Years Later: A Comparison Between Census Studies of Patients in Psychiatric Institutions in Denmark in 1957 and 1962. *Acta Jutland* 35: No. 1, Med. Ser. 13, 1963.
152. Kallmann, F. J.: The Genetics of Psychoses: An Analysis of 1,232 Twin Index Families (Congrès International de Psychiatrie, VI, Paris, 1950). Also published as Genetic Aspects of Psychoses, chapter19 in *The Biology of Mental Health and*

Disease (The Twenty-seventh Annual Conference of the Milbank Memorial Fund). New York: Paul B. Hoeber, 1952.
153. Kallmann, F. J.: Genetic Principles in Manic-Depressive Psychosis. In *Depression,* ed. P. H. Hoch and J. Zubin. New York: Grune & Stratton, 1954.
154. Kallmann, F. J.: An Appraisal of Psychogenetic Twin Data. *Dis. Nerv.* System (Suppl.) 19:9, 1958.
155. Kardiner, A.: The Relation of Culture to Mental Disorder. In *Current Problems in Psychiatric Diagnosis,* ed. P. H. Hoch and J. Zubin. New York: Grune & Stratton, 1953.
156. Karlsson, K. W.: Migration and Mental Illness in Helsinki. Sixth World Congress of Psychiatry, Madrid, Spain, September 5–11, 1966. *Abstracts, International Congress Series No. 117,* p. 250. Amsterdam: Excerpta Medica Foundation, 1966.
157. Katchadourian, H.: The Prevalence of Mental Illness Among the Christians and Moslems of Lebanon. Sixth World Congress of Psychiatry, Madrid, Spain, September 5–11, 1966. *Abstracts, International Congress Series No. 117,* p. 250. Amsterdam: Excerpta Medica Foundation, 1966.
158. Katz, M. M., Cole, J. O., and Lowery, H. A.: Studies of the Diagnostic Process: The Influence of Symptom Perception, Past Experience and Ethnic Background on Diagnostic Decisions. *Amer. J. Psychiat.,* in press.
159. Keeler, R.: Children's Reaction to the Death of a Parent. In *Depression,* ed. P. H. Hoch and J. Zubin. New York: Grune & Stratton, 1954.
160. Kessel, W. I. N.: Psychiatric Morbidity in a London General Practice. *Brit. J. Prev. Soc. Med.* 14:16, 1960.
161. Kety, S. S.: In *Antidepressant Drugs of the Non-MAO Inhibitor Type,* Washington, D. C., ed. S. S. Kety and D. H. Efron. Workshop Series of Pharmacology Unit, National Institute of Mental Health, No. 1, January 27–28, 1966, Public Health Service, U.S. Department of Health, Education, and Welfare.
162. Kiloh, L. G., and Garside, R. F.: The Independence of Neurotic Depression and Endogenous Depression. *Brit. J. Psychiat.* 109:451–63, July 1963.
163. Klee, G. D., Spiro, E., Bahn, A. K., and Gorwitz, K.: An Ecological Analysis of Diagnosed Mental Illness in Baltimore. In *Psychiatric Epidemiology and Mental Health Planning,* ed. R. R. Monroe, G. D. Klee, and E. G. Brody. Washington, D.C.: Psychiatric Research Report 22, American Psychiatric Association, April 1967.

164. Klein, M.: A Contribution of the Psychogenesis of Manic-depressive States. *Int. Psychoanal.* 16:145–94, 1935.
165. Klein, M.: Mourning, Its Relation to Manic-Depressive States, 1940. In *Contributions to Psychoanalysis*, 1921–1945. London: Hogarth Press, 1948.
166. Kohn, M. L.: Social Class and Schizophrenia: A Critical Review. Presented to Foundations' Fund for Research in Psychiatry Conference on the Transmission of Schizophrenia, San Juan, Puerto Rico, June 1967.
167. Kraepelin, E.: *Lectures on Clinical Psychiatry*, Ed. 3. Translation from the second German edition (rev. and ed. T. Johnstone). New York: William Wood, 1917.
168. Kraepelin, E.: Manic-Depressive Insanity and Paranoia, (trans. R. M. Barclay, ed. G. M. Robertson). Edinburgh: E. & S. Livingston, 1921.
169. Kraines, S. H.: *Mental Depressions and Their Treatment*. New York: The Macmillan Co., 1957.
170. Kramer, M.: Some Problems for International Research Suggested by Observations on Differences in First Admission Rates to the Mental Hospitals of England and Wales and of the United States. Proceedings Third World Congress of Psychiatry, Montreal, Canada, 1961, pp. 153–160.
171. Kramer, M.: Classification of Mental Disorders. Presented at Conference on the Role and Methodology of Classification in Psychiatry and Psychopathology, Washington, D.C., November 19–21, 1965.
172. Kramer, M.: *Some Implications of Trends in the Usage of Psychiatric Facilities for Community Mental Health Programs and Related Research*. National Institute of Mental Health, U.S. Dept. of Health, Education, and Welfare, PHS. Washington, D.C.: Public Health Service Publication No. 1434, 1966.
173. Kramer, M., Pollack, E. S., and Redick, R. W.: Studies of the Incidence and Prevalence of Hospitalized Mental Disorders in the United States: Current Status and Future Goals. In *Comparative Epidemiology of the Mental Disorders*, ed. P H. Hoch and J. Zubin, pp. 56–100. New York.: Grune & Stratton, 1961.
174. Kretschmer, E.: Heredity and Constitution in Aetiology of Psychic Disorders. *Brit. Med. J.* 2:403–06, 1937.
175. Langner, T. S., and Michael, S. T.: *Life Stress and Mental Health: The Midtown Manhattan Study*. New York: Free Press, 1963.

176. Lapouse, R.: Problems in Studying the Prevalence of Psychiatric Disorders. *Amer. J. Public Health* 57:947–54, June 1967.
177. Lascelles, R. G.: Atypical Facial Pain and Depression *Brit. J. Psychiat.* 112:651–59, 1966.
178. Lebovits, B. Z., Shekelle, R. B., Ostfeld, A.M., and Paul, O.: Prospective and Retrospective Psychological Studies of Coronary Heart Disease. *Psychosom. Med.* 29:265–72, 1967.
179. Lehmann, H. E.: Depressions: Categories, Mechanisms and Phenomena. In *Pharmacotherapy of Depression*, ed. J. O. Cole and J. R. W. Herborn. Springfield, Ill.: Chas. C Thomas, 1966.
180. Lehmann, H. E.: Facts v. Fallacies in the Overall Treatment of Depression. 1967 Winter Symposium on Mental Depression. Washington Psychiatric Society and Department of Psychiatry, Georgetown University School of Medicine, Washington, D.C., March 12, 1967.
181. Leighton, A. H.: *My Name is Legion*. The Stirling County Study of Psychiatric Disorder and Sociocultural Environment, Vol. 1. New York: Basic Books, 1959.
182. Leighton, A. H., Lambo, T. A., Hughes, C. C., Leighton, D. C., Murphy, J. M., and Macklin, D. B.: *Psychiatric Disorder Among the Yoruba*. Ithaca, N.Y.: Cornell University Press, 1963.
183. Leighton, D. C., Harding, J. S., Macklin, D. B., MacMillan, A. M., and Leighton, A. H.: *The Character of Danger: Psychiatric Symptoms in Selected Communities*. The Stirling County Study of Psychiatric Disorder and Sociocultural Environment, Vol. 3. New York: Basic Books, 1963.
184. Lemkau, P. V.: The Epidemiological Study of Mental Illness and Mental Health. *Amer. J. Psychiat.* 111:801–9, May 1955.
185. Lemkau, P. V., Tietze, C., and Cooper, M.: Mental Hygiene Problems in an Urban District. I. Description of the Study. *Mental Hyg.* 25:624–46, October 1941.
186. Lemkau, P. V., Tietze, C., and Cooper, M.: Mental Hygiene Problems in an Urban District. II. The Psychotics and the Neurotics. *Mental Hyg.* 26:100–19, January 1942.
187. Lemkau, P. V., Tietze, C., and Cooper, M.: Complaint of Nervousness and the Psychoneuroses: An Epidemiological Viewpoint. *Amer. J. Orthopsychiat.* 12:214–23, April 1942.
188. Lemkau, P. V., Tietze, C., and Cooper, M.: A Survey of Statistical Studies on the Prevalence and Incidence of Mental

Disorder in Sample Populations. *Public Health Rep.* 58:1909, December 31, 1943.
189. Lendrum, F. C.: A Thousand Cases of Attempted Suicide. *Amer. J. Psychiat.* 13:479–500, November 1933.
190. Lewin, B. D.: *The Psychoanalysis of Elation.* New York: W. W. Norton, 1950.
191. Lewin, K. K.: Role of Depression in the Production of Illness in Pernicious Anemia. *Psychosom. Med.* 21: 23–27, 1959.
192. Lewis, A. J.: Melancholia: A Historical Review. *J. Ment. Sci.* 80:1, 1934.
193. Lewis, A. J.: In *Field Studies in the Mental Disorders,* ed. J. Zubin, p. 257. New York: Grune & Stratton, 1961.
194. Lewis, A. J.: Fertility and Mental Illness. *Eugenics Rev.* 50:91–106, 1958.
195. Lewis, A. J.: General Review of Depressive Conditions. In Davies, E. B., ed.: *Depression.* Cambridge: Cambridge University Press, 1964.
196. Lewis, N. D. C., and Piotrowski, Z. A.: Clinical Diagnosis of Manic-Depressive Psychosis. In *Depression,* ed. P. H. Hoch, and J. Zubin. New York: Grune & Stratton, 1954.
197. Lilienfeld, A. M.: Epidemiological Methods and Inferences in Studies of Noninfectious Diseases. *Public Health Rep.* 72:51–60, 1957.
198. Lilienfeld, A. M.: A Methodological Problem in Testing a Recessive Genetic Hypothesis in Human Disease. *Amer. J. Public Health.* 49:199–204. February 1959.
199. Lin, T.: A Study of the Incidence of Mental Disorders in Chinese and Other Cultures. *Psychiatry* 16:313–36, 1953.
200. Lin, T.: The Epidemiological Study of Mental Disorders by World Health Organization. *Soc. Psychiat.* 1:204–06, March 1967.
201. Lin, T., and Standley, C. C.: *The Scope of Epidemiology in Psychiatry.* Public Health Papers no. 16. Geneva: World Health Organization, 1962.
202. Lindemann, E.: Symptomatology and Management of Acute Grief. *Amer. J. Psychiat.* 101:141, 1944.
203. Lindemann, E.: Mental Health—Fundamental to a Dynamic Epidemiology of Health. In *The Epidemiology of Health,* ed. I. Galdston. New York: Health Educational Council, 1953.
204. Locke, B. Z., Finucane, D. L., and Hassler, F.: Emotionally Disturbed Patients Under Care of Private Non-Psychiatric Physicians. In *Psychiatric Epidemiology and Mental Health*

Planning, ed. R. R. Monroe, G. D. Klee, and E. B. Brody. Psychiatric Research Reports of the American Psychiatric Association no. 22, April 1967.
205. Lourie, R. S.: Suicide and Attempted Suicide in Children and Adolescents. In *Symposium on Suicide,* ed. L. Yochelson. The George Washington University School of Medicine, Department of Psychiatry, Washington, D.C., 1965.
206. Lubin, B.: Adjective Checklists for Measurement of Depression. *Arch. Gen. Psychiat.* 12:57–62, January 1965.
207. Luxenburger, H.: Demographische und psychiatriche Untersuchungen in der engeren biologischen Familie von Paralytikerhegatten. Z. ges. Neurol. Psychiat. 112:331–491, 1928.
208. Lyerly, S. B., and Abbot, P. S.: *Handbook of Psychiatric Rating Scales* (1959–1964). Washington, D.C.: National Institute of Mental Health. Public Health Service Publication no. 1495, 1966.
209. MacKinnon, P. C. B., and MacKinnon, I. L.: Hazards of the Menstrual Cycle. *Brit. Med. J.,* 1:555, 1956.
210. MacMahon, B., Johnson, S., and Pugh, T. F.: Relation of Suicide Rates to Social Conditions. *Public Health Rep.* 78:285–93, April 1963.
211. MacMahon, B., Pugh, T. F., and Ipsen, J.: *Epidemiologic Methods.* Boston: Little, Brown & Co., 1960.
212. Malzberg, B.: *Social and Biological Aspects of Mental Disease.* Utica, N.Y.: State Hospitals Press, 1940.
213. Malzberg, B.: Distribution of Mental Disease in New York State, 1949–1951. *Psychiat. Quart.* (Suppl.) 29:209–38, 1955.
214. Malzberg, B.: Important Statistical Data About Mental Illness. In *American Handbook of Psychiatry,* Vol. 1, ed. S. Arieti, p. 161. New York: Basic Books, 1959.
215. Malzberg, B., and Lee, E. S.: *Migration and Mental Disease. A Study of First Admissions to Hospitals for Mental Disease, New York 1939–1941.* New York: Social Science Research Council, 1956.
216. Maoz, M. D., Levy, S., Brand, N., and Halevi, H. S.: An Epidemiological Survey of Mental Disorders in a Community of Newcomers to Israel. *J. Coll. Gen. Practit.* 11:267–84, 1966.
217. Martin, F. M., Brotherston, J. H. F., and Chave, S. P. W.: The Incidence of Neurosis in a New Housing Estate. *Brit. J. Prev. Soc. Med.* 11:196, 1957.
218. Mazer, M.: A Psychiatric and Parapsychiatric Register for an

Island Community. *Arch. Gen. Psychiat.* 14:366–71, April 1966.
219. Mazer, M.: Personal communication.
220. Mayer-Gross, W., Slater, E., and Roth, M.: *Clinical Psychiatry.* Baltimore: The Williams & Wilkins Co., 1960.
221. McCarthy, P. D., and Walsh, D.: Suicide in Dublin. *Brit. Med. J.* 1:1393–96, 1966.
222. McGough, W. E., Williams, E., and Blackley, J.: Changing Patterns of Psychiatric Illness Among Negroes of the Southern United States. Sixth World Congress of Psychiatry, Madrid, Spain, September 5–11, 1966. *Abstracts, International Congress Series No. 117.* Amsterdam: Excerpta Medica Foundation, 1966, pp. 304–5.
223. Mendelson, M.: *Psychoanalytic Concepts of Depression.* Springfield, Ill.: Chas. C Thomas, 1960.
224. Menninger, K.: *The Vital Balance.* New York: The Viking Press, 1963.
225. Merrell, D. H.: Inheritance of Manic-Depressive Psychosis. *A. M. A. Arch. Neurol. Psychiat.* 66:272–79, 1951.
226. Meyer, A.: *Periodicity. Collected Papers.* Baltimore: The Johns Hopkins Press, 1951.
227. Meyer, A.: Psychobiology. In *A Science of Man,* ed. E. E. Winters and A. M. Bowers. Springfield, Ill.: Chas. C Thomas, 1957.
228. Michael, R. P., and Gibbons, J. L.: Interrelationships Between the Endocrine System and Neuropsychiatry. In *International Review of Neurobiology,* ed. C. Pfeifer and J. Smythies, pp. 243–302. New York: Academic Press, 1963.
229. Mishler, E. G., and Scotch, N. A.: Sociocultural Factors in the Epidemiology of Schizophrenia: A Review. *Psychiatry,* 26:315–51, 1963.
230. Montagu, A.: Culture and Mental Illness. Presented at 1967 Winter Symposium on Mental Depression. Washington Psychiatric Society and Department of Psychiatry, Georgetown University School of Medicine, Washington, D.C., March 12, 1967.
231. Morivama. I. M.: The Eighth Revision of the International Classification of Diseases. *Amer. J. Public Health.* 56:1277–80, August 1966.
232. Morris, J. N.: *Uses of Epidemiology.* Baltimore: The Williams & Wilkins Co., 1964.
233. Muncie, W.: The Psychobiological Approach. In *American*

Handbook of Psychiatry, Vol. 2, ed. S. Arieti. New York: Basic Books, 1959.
234. Munro, A.: Depressive Illness in Twins. *Acta Psychiat. Scand.* 41:111–16, 1965.
235. Munro, A.: Parental Deprivation in Depressive Patients. *Brit. J. Psychiat.* 112:443–57, 1966.
236. Murphy, H. B. M.: Migration and the Major Mental Disorders: A Reappraisal. In *Mobility and Mental Health*, ed. M. B. Kantor, p. 5–29. Springfield, Ill.: Chas. C Thomas, 1965.
237. Murphy, H. B. M., Wittkower, E. D., and Chance, N.: A Crosscultural Inquiry Into the Symptomatology of Depression: A Preliminary Report. *Int. J. Psychiat.* 3:6–22, January 1967.
238. National Institute of Mental Health. Ad Hoc Committee on Epidemiology, October 4–5, 1966. Proceedings unpublished.
239. National Institute of Mental Health, Biometry Branch, Public Health Service, U.S. Dept. of Health, Education and Welfare. Unpublished data.
240. National Institute of Mental Health, Research Utilization Conference Series: Conference on the Epidemiology of Mental Disorders, June 21–22, 1965. Unpublished.
241. Nielsen, J., Juel-Nielsen, N., and Strömgren, E.; A Five-Year Survey of a Psychiatric Service in a Geographically Delimited Rural Population Given Access to this Service. *Comprehensive Psychiat.* 6:139–65, 1965.
242. Norris, V.: *Mental Illness in London.* Maudsley Monograph No. 6. London: Chapman and Hall, Ltd., 1959.
243. Ödegaard, O.: Emigration and Insanity. *Acta Psychiat. & Neurolog.*, Suppl. 4, 1932.
244. Ödegaard, O.: Marriage and Mental Disease. A Study in Social Psychopathology. *J. Ment. Sci.* 92:35–59, 1946.
245. Ödegaard, O.: The Incidence of Mental Diseases as Measured by Census Investigation versus Admission Statistics. *Psychiat. Quart.* 26:212–18, 1952.
246. Ödegaard, O.: New Data on Marriage and Mental Disease. Incidence of Psychoses in Widowed and Divorced. *J. Ment. Sci.* 99:778–85, 1953.
247. Ödegaard, O.: The Epidemiology of Depressive Psychoses. *Acta Psychiat. Scand.* Suppl. 162, 37:33–38, 1961.
248. Ödegaard, O.: Occupational Incidence of Mental Disease in Single Women. *Living Conditions and Health,* 1:169–80, 1957.

249. Oltman, J. E., and Friedman, S.: Trends in Admissions to a State Hospital. *Arch. Gen. Psychiat.* 13:744–51, 1965.
250. O'Neal, P., Robins, E., and Schmidt, E. H.: A Psychiatric Study of Attempted Suicide in Persons Over Sixty Years of Age. *Arch. Neurol. Psychiat.* 75:275–84, 1956.
251. Overall, J. E., Hollister, L. E., Pokorny, A. D., Casey, J. F., and Katz, G.: Drug Therapy in Depression. *Clin. Pharmacol. Therapeut.* 3:16–22, 1962.
252. Paffenbarger, R. S.: The Picture Puzzle of the Postpartum Psychoses. *J. Chronic Dis.* 13:161, 1961.
253. Paffenbarger, R. S.: Epidemiological Aspects of Parapartum Mental Illness. *Brit. J. Prev. Soc. Med.* 18:189–95, 1964.
254. Paffenbarger, R. S., and Asnes, D. P.: Chronic Disease in Former College Students. III. Precursors of Suicide in Early and Middle Life. *Amer. J. Public Health.* 56:1026–36, July 1966.
255. Paffenbarger, R. S., and McCabe, L. J.: The Effect of Obstetric and Perinatal Events on Risk of Mental Illness in Women of Childbearing Age. *Amer. J. Public Health,* 56:400–7, March 1966.
256. Panum, P. L.: *Panum on Measles: Observations Made During the Epidemic of Measles on the Faroe Islands in the Year 1846,* pp. 13–14. Delta Omega Society, 1940. Distributed by the American Public Health Association, 1790 Broadway, New York, N.Y.
257. Pasamanick, B., Dinitz, S., and Lefton, L.: Psychiatric Orientation and Its Relation to Diagnosis and Treatment in a Mental Hospital. *Amer. J. Psychiat.* 116:127, 1959.
258. Piers, G. and Singer, M. B.: *Shame and Guilt: A Psychoanalytic and a Cultural Study.* Springfield, Ill.: Chas. C Thomas, 1953.
259. Pitts, F. W., Meyer, J., Brooks, M., and Winokur, G.: Adult Psychiatric Illness Assessed for Childhood Parental Loss, and Psychiatric Illness in Family Members—a Study of 748 Patients and 250 Controls. *Amer. J. Psychiat.* 121, No. 12: Supp. 1–10, 1965.
260. Plunkett, R. J., and Gordon, J. E.: *Epidemiology and Mental Illness.* New York: Basic Books, 1960.
261. Plunkett, R. J., and Hayden, A. B., ed.: *American Medical Association. Standard Nomenclature of Diseases and Operations,* 4th ed. New York: Blakiston, 1952.
262. Pollock, H. M.: Prevalence of Manic-Depressive Psychoses in Relation to Sex, Age, Environment, Nativity and Race.

Manic-Depressive Psychosis, vol. 2 of the Association for Research in Nervous and Mental Disease. Baltimore: The Williams & Wilkens Co., 1931.
263. Pollock, H. M.: Development of Statistics of Mental Disease in U. S. During Past Century. *Amer. J. Psychiat.* 102:1–17, July 1945.
264. Pollock, H. M., Malzberg, B., and Fuller, R. G.: Hereditary and Environmental Factors in the Causation of Manic-Depressive Psychoses and Dementia Praecox. Utica, N.Y.: State Hospitals Press, 1939. *Amer. J. Psychiat.* 96:1227–44, 1940.
265. Powell, G. F., Brasel, J. A., and Blizzard, R. M.: Emotional Deprivation and Growth Retardation Simulating Idiopathic Hypopituitarism. I. Clinical Evaluation of the Syndrome. II. (with Raiti, S.) Endocrinologic Evaluation of the Syndrome. *New Eng. J. Med.* 276:1271–83, 1967.
266. Pugh, T. F., Jerath, B. K., Schmidt, W. M., and Reed, R. B.: Rates of Mental Disease Related to Childbearing. *New Eng. J. Med.* 266:1224–28, May 30, 1963.
267. Pugh, T. F., and MacMahon, B.: *Epidemiological Findings in U. S. Mental Hospital Data.* Boston: Little, Brown, 1962.
268. Pyke, D. A.: Finger Clubbing: Validity as a Physical Sign. *Lancet* 267:352-54, Aug. 21, 1954.
269. Rado, S.: Psychodynamics of Depression from the Etiologic Point of View. Psychosom. Med. 13:51, January & February 1951.
270. Rao, V.: Depression in Southern India. Sixth World Congress of Psychiatry, Madrid, Spain, September 5–11, 1966. *Abstracts, International Congress Series No. 117.* Amsterdam: Excerpta Medica Foundation, 1966.
271. Rawnsley, K., and Loudon, J. B.: Factors Influencing the Referral of Patients to Psychiatrists by General Practitioners. *Brit. J. Prev. Soc. Med.* 16:174–81, 1962.
272. Redlich, F. C., and Freedman, D. X.: *The Theory and Practice of Psychiatry.* New York: Basic Books, Inc., 1966.
273. Rees, L.: Constitutional Factors and Abnormal Behavior. In *Handbook of Abnormal Psychology,* ed. H. J. Eysenck. New York: Basic Books, 1960.
274. Reid, D. D.: Epidemiological Methods in the Study of Mental Disorders. Public Health Papers No. 2. Geneva: World Health Organization, 1960.
275. Reid, D. D.: Precipitating Proximal Factors in the Occurrence of Mental Disorders: Epidemiological Evidence. In

Causes of Mental Disorders: A Review of Epidemiological Knowledge, 1959. New York: Milbank Memorial Fund, 1961.
276. Rennie, T. A.: Prognosis in Manic-depressive Psychosis. *Amer. J. Psychiat.* 98:801–14, May 1942.
277. Rennie, T. A. Prognosis in the Psychoneuroses: Benign and Malignant Developments. In *Current Problems in Psychiatric Diagnosis,* ed. P. H. Hoch and J. Zubin, pp. 66–79. New York: Grune & Stratton, 1953.
278. Richter, C. P.: *Biological Clocks in Medicine and Psychiatry.* Springfield, Ill.: Chas. C Thomas, 1965.
279. Rin, H., and Lin, T.: Mental Illness Among Formosan Aborigines as Compared with the Chinese in Taiwan. *J. Ment. Sci.* 108:134–46, 1962.
280. Roberts, B. H., and Myers, J. K.: Religion, National Origin, Immigration, and Mental Illness. *Amer. J. Psychiat.* 110:759–64, April 1954.
281. Robins, E., Murphy, G. E., Wilkinson, R. H., Glassner, S., and Kayes, J.: Some Clinical Considerations in the Prevention of Suicide Based on a Study of 134 Successful Suicides. Amer. J. Public Health 49:888-98, 1959.
282. Rogers, M. E., Lilienfeld, A. M., and Pasamanick, B.: Prenatal and Paranatal Factors in the Development of Childhood Behavior Disorders. *Acta Psychiat. Neurol. Scand.,* Suppl. 102:1–81, 1955.
283. Rosanoff, A. J., Handy, L. M., and Plesset, I. R.: The Etiology of Manic-Depressive Syndromes with Special Reference to their Occurrence in Twins. *Amer. J. Psychiat.* 91:725-62, 1935.
284. Rose, A. M.: The Prevalence of Mental Disorders in Italy. *Int. J. Soc. Psychiat.* 10:87–100, 1964.
285. Rosen, B. M., Bahn, A. K., and Kramer, M.: Demographic and Diagnostic Characteristics of Psychiatric Clinic Outpatients in the USA, 1961. *Amer. J. Orthopsychiat.* 34:455–68, 1964.
286. Rosenthal, D.: Discussion. *Int. J. Psychiat.,* 1:480–81, 1965.
287. Rosenthal, S. H.: Changes in a Population of Hospitalized Patients with Affective Disorders, 1945–1965. *Amer. J. Psychiat.* 123:6, December 1966.
288. Roth, M.: The Phenomenology of Depressive States. *Canad. Psychiat. Ass. J.* 4 (Special Suppl.): S32–S54, 1959.
289. Roth, W. F., and Luton, F. H.: Mental Health Program in Tennessee. *Amer. J. Psychiat.* 99:662–75, 1943.

290. Royes, K.: The Incidence and Features of Psychoses in a Carribean Community. In *Proceedings of Third World Congress of Psychiatry,* Vol. II, pp. 1121–25. Montreal, Canada, June 4–10, 1961.
291. Ryle, A.: Psychoses in General Practice: An Epidemiological Survey. *J. Mont. Sci.* 107:1020–27, November 1961.
292. Sainsbury, P.: *Suicide in London: An Ecological Study.* New York: Basic Books, 1956.
293. Sainsbury, P.: Suicide in Later Life. *Geront. Clin.* 4:161–70, 1962.
294. Salk, L.: Thoughts on the Concept of Imprinting and Its Place in Early Human Development. Panel V—On the Depressive Illnesses in Childhood. Canad. Psychiat. Ass. J. 11: special supplement, 1966.
295. Sartwell, P.: Epidemiology. In: Maxcy-Rosenau—*Preventive Medicine and Public Health,* 9th Ed., ed. P. Sartwell, pp. 1–19. New York: Appleton-Century-Crofts, 1965.
296. Sshildkraut, J. J.: The Catecholamine Hypothesis of Affective Disorders: A Review of Supporting Evidence. *Amer. J. Psychiat.* 122:509–22, November 1965.
297. Schildkraut, J. J., Schanberg, S. M., Breese, G. R., and Kopin, I. J.: Norepinephrine Metabolism and Drugs Used in the Affective Disorders: A Possible Mechanism of Action. *Amer. J. Psychiat.* 124:600–08, November 1967.
298. Schmale, A. H., Jr.: Relationship of Separation and Depression to Disease. I. A Report on a Hospitalized Medical Population. *Psychosom. Med.* 20:259–77, 1958.
299. Schmidt, H. O., and Fonda, C. P.: The Reliability of Psychiatric Diagnosis: A New Look. *J. Abnorm. Soc. Psychol.* 52:262–67, 1956.
300. Schroeder, C. W.: Mental Disorders in Cities. *Amer. J. Sociol.* 48:40–47, July 1942.
301. Schwab, J. J., Clemmons, R. S., Bialow, B., Duggan, V., and Davis, B.: A Study of the Somatic Symptomatology of Depression in Medical Inpatients. *Psychosomatics* 6:273–77, 1965.
302. Seager, C. P., and Flood, R. A.: Suicide in Bristol. *Brit. J. Psychiat.* 111:919–32, October 1965.
303. Shaw, B.: Preface on Doctors, *The Doctor's Dilemma.* New York: Brentano's, 1911.
304. Sheldon, W. H., Stevens, S. S., and Tucker, W. B.: *The Varieties of Human Physique: An Introduction to Constitutional Psychology.* New York: Stechert-Hagner, Inc., 1940.

305. Shepherd, M., Fisher, M., Stein, L., and Kessel, W. I. N.: Psychiatric Morbidity in an Urban Group Practice. *Proc. Royal Soc. Med.* 52:269–74, 1959.
306. Shields, J.: Personality Differences and Neurotic Traits in Normal Twin School Children. A Study in Psychiatric Genetics. *Eugenics Rev.* 45:213–46, 1954.
307. Shneidman, E. S., and Farberow, N. L.: Clues to Suicide. *Public Health Rep.* 7:109–14, Feb. 1956.
308. Simon, R.: Involutional Psychosis in Negroes. *A. M. A. Arch. Gen. Psychiat.* 13:148–54, August 1965.
309. Sjögren, T.: Genetic-Statistical and Psychiatric Investigations of a West Swedish Population. *Acta Psychiat. Neurolog.,* Suppl. 52, 1948.
310. Slater, E.: The Incidence of Mental Disorder. *Ann. Eugenics* 6:172–86, 1935.
311. Slater, E.: The Inheritance of Manic-Depressive Insanity and Its Relation to Mental Defect. *J. Ment. Sci.* 82:626, 1936.
312. Slater, E.: Zur Erbpathologie des Manisch-Depressiven Irreseins: Die Eltern und Kindern von Manish-Depressiven. *Zt. ges. Neurol. Psychiat.* 163:1–47, 1938.
313. Slater, E.: *Psychotic and Neurotic Illnesses in Twins.* Medical Research Council Special Report Series No. 278. London: Her Majesty's Stationery Office, 1953.
314. Smith, R. T.: A Comparison of Socioenvironmental Factors in Monozygotic and Dizygotic Twins, Testing an Assumption. In *Methods and Goals in Human Behavior Genetics,* ed.: S. G. Vandenberg. New York: Academic Press, 1965.
315. Sommer, C., and Harman, H. H.: Trend in Mental Diseases in Illinois—1922–1943. In: American Psychopathological Association: *Trends in Mental Diseases.* New York: Columbia University Press, 1945.
316. Sørensen, A., and Strömgren, E.: Frequency of Depressive States Within Geographically Delimited Population Groups. 2. Prevalence (The Samsø Investigation). *Acta Psychiat. Scand.* 37, Suppl. 162:62–68, 1961.
317. Spitz, R. A.: Anaclitic Depression. *Psychoanalyt. Study of Child* 2:313–41, 1946.
318. Spitz, R. A.: *Hospitalism: An Inquiry Into the Genesis of Psychiatric Conditions in Early Childhood.* New York: International Universities Press, 1945.
319. Srole, L., Langner, T. S., Michael, S. T., Opler, M. K., and Rennie, T. A. C.: *Mental Health in the Metropolis: The Midtown Manhattan Study.* New York: McGraw-Hill, 1962.

320. Stainbrook, E.: A Cross-Cultural Evaluation of Depressive Reactions. In *Depression,* ed. P. H. Hoch and J. Zubin. New York: Grune & Stratton, 1954.
321. Stearns, A. W.: Suicide in Massachusetts. *Mental Hygiene,* 5:752–77, October 1921.
322. Stengel, E., and Cook, N. G.: *Attempted Suicide.* Maudsley Monograph no. 4. London: Chapman and Hall, 1958.
323. Stengel, E.: Classification of Mental Disorders. *Bull. WHO* 21:601–63, 1960.
324. Stengel, E.: Recent Research Into Suicide and Attempted Suicide. *Amer. J. Psychiat.,* 118:725–27, February 1962.
325. Stenstedt, A.: Study in Manic-Depressive Psychosis: Clinical, Social and Genetic Investigations. *Acta Psychiat. Neurolog. Scand.* Suppl. 79:1–111, 1952.
326. Stenstedt, A.: Involutional Melancholia: An Etiological, Clinical and Social Study of Endogenous Depression in Later Life, with Special Reference to Genetic Factors. *Acta Psychiat. Neurolog. Scand.* 34, Suppl. 127:1–71 1959.
327. Strömgren, E.: Social Surveys. *J. Ment. Sci.* 94:266–76, 1948.
328. Stunkard, A. J.: The "Dieting Depression." *Amer. J. Med.* 23:77–86, 1957.
329. Szalita, A. B.: Psychodynamics of Disorders of the Involutional Age. In *American Handbook of Psychiatry,* Vol. 3, ed. S. Arieti. New York: Basic Books, 1966.
330. Tabachnik, N. D., and Farberow, N. L.: The Assessment of Self-destructive Potentiality. In *The Cry for Help,* ed. N.L. Farberow and E. S. Shneidman. New York: McGraw-Hill, 1961.
331. Taylor, L., and Chave, S.: *Mental Health and Environment.* Boston: Little, Brown & Co., 1964.
332. Temoche, A., Pugh, T. F., and MacMahon, B.: Suicide Rates Among Current and Former Mental Institution Patients. *J. Nerv. and Ment. Dis.,* 138:124, February 1964.
333. Terris, M.: Use of Hospital Admissions in Epidemiological Studies of Mental Disease. *Arch. Gen. Psychiat.* 12:420–26, April 1965.
334. Tienari, P.: Psychiatric Illnesses in Identical Twins. *Acta Psychiat. Scand.* Suppl. 171, 39:1–195, 1963.
335. Tietze, C., Lemkau, P. V., and Cooper, M.: Schizophrenia, Manic-Depressive Psychosis and Social-Economic Status. *Amer. J. Social.* 47:167–75, 1941–1942.
336. Tod, E. D.: Puerperal Depression: A Prospective Epidemiological Study. *Lancet* 2:1264–66, 1964.

SELECTED BIBLIOGRAPHY

337. Tonks, C. M., Rack, P., and Rose, M. J.: Attempted Suicide and Menstruation. Sixth World Congress of Psychiatry, Madrid, Spain, September 5–11, 1966. *Abstracts, International Congress Series No. 117*, p. 414. Amsterdam: Excerpta Medica Foundation, 1966.
338. Torrey, E. F., ed.: *An Introduction to Health and Health Education in Ethiopia.* Addis Ababa: Berhanena Selam Printing Press, 1966.
339. U.S. Department of Health, Education, and Welfare, Public Health Service, National Institutes of Health, National Institute of Mental Health. *Patients in Mental Institutions, 1965: Part II.* State and County Mental Hospitals. Part III. Private Mental Hospitals and General Hospitals with Psychiatric Facilities. PHS Publication No. 1597.
340. U.S. Department of Health, Education, and Welfare, Public Health Service, National Center for Health Statistics. *Suicide in the United States 1950–1964.* PHS Publication No. 1,000, Series 20, No. 5, August 1967.
341. U.S. Department of Health, Education, and Welfare, Public Health Service, National Center for Health Statistics. *Mortality Trends in the United States 1954–1963.* PHS Publication No. 1,000, Series 20, No. 2, June 1966.
342. Wagner, P. S.: A Comparative Study of Negro and White Admissions to the Psychiatric General Hospital. *Amer. J. Psychiat.* 95:167–83, 1938.
343. Ward, C. H., Beck, A. T., Mendelson, M., Mock, J. E., and Erbaugh, J. K.: The Psychiatric Nomenclature: Reasons for Diagnostic Disagreement. *Arch. Gen. Psychiat.* 7:198–205, 1962.
344. Wechsler, H.: Community Growth, Depressive Disorders and Suicide. *Amer. J. Sociol.* 67:9–16, 1961.
345. Weinberg, S. K.: Cultural Aspects of Manic-Depression in West Africa. *J. Health and Human Behav.* 6:247–53, 1965.
346. Weinberg, W.: Zur Korrektur des Einflusses der Lebensdauer und Todesauslese auf die Ergebnisse bestimmter Kreuzungen. *Arch. Rassen. Gesellschafts—biologie* 11:434–44, 1915.
347. Whitehorn, J. C.: Observations on Clinical and Diagnostic Problems of Depressions. Presented at National Institute of Mental Health Conference on the Epidemiology of Mental Disorders, Bethesda, Md., June 21-22, 1965.
348. Whitwell, J. R.: *Historical Notes on Psychiatry.* London: John Lewis, 1936.
349. Winn, D., and Halla, R.: Observations of Children Who

Threaten To Kill Themselves. Panel V—On the Depressive Illnesses in Childhood. *Canad. Psychiat. Ass. J.* 11 (special supplement): 1966.

350. Winokur, G., and Pitts, F. N., Jr.: Affective Disorder: VI. A Family History Study of Prevalences, Sex Differences and Possible Genetic Factors. *J. Psychiat. Res.* 3:113–23, August 1965.
351. Wittkower, E. D., and Rin, H.: Transcultural Psychiatry. *Arch. Gen.* Psychiat. 13:387, November 1965.
352. World Health Organization: *Deprivation of Maternal Care: A Reassessment of its Effects* (Public Health Papers No. 14) Geneva: WHO, 1962.
353. Yolles, S. F., and Kramer, M.: Vital Statistics of Schizophrenia. Submitted as a chapter for the revised edition of *Schizophrenia: A Review of the Syndrome,* to be edited by L. Bellak, and L. Loeb.
354. Yoo, P. S.: Mental Disorders in Korean Rural Communities. Proceedings of the Third World Congress of Psychiatry, Montreal, Canada, June 4–10, 1961, pp. 1305–9.
355. Zilboorg, G.: Manic-Depressive Psychoses. In *Psychoanalysis Today: Its Scope and Function,* ed. S. Lorand, pp. 224–45. New York: Covici, Friede, 1933.
356. Zilboorg, G.: *A History of Medical Psychology.* New York: Norton, 1966.
357. Zubin, J., ed.: *Field Studies in Mental Disorders.* New York: Grune & Stratton, 1961.
358. Zung, W. K.: A Self-Rating Depression Scale. *Arch. Gen. Psychiat.* 12:63–70, January 1965.

INDEX

Addison's disease, 107, 114
Adrenal hormones, 106–7
Adrenocortical insufficiency, 107, 114
Affective (cyclothymic) personality disorders, definition, 10
Affective disorders, definition, 9
Africa, depression in, 82
Age: variations in, and depression, 78–80; and suicide rates, 57
Aggression, 126
Alcoholic psychosis, 83; and suicide, 65, 67, (*table*) 68
American Medical Association, 13
American Psychiatric Association (APA), 7, 12–13

Amines, decrease of, and depression, 105
Anaclitic depression, 78
Anorexia nervosa, 112
Antidepressant drugs, 93–94, 105
Anxiety, 5, 7
Attempted suicide, 14, 60, 69–71, 79

Behavior genetics, 97–98
Benzedrine, 114
Biochemical factors, depression and mania, 105–8
Biologic clocks, 110
Biometrics Branch (National Insti-

tute of Mental Health), 28–29, 52
Bureau of Census (U.S.), 28

Catecholamine metabolism, 105–6
Cerebral arteriosclerosis, and suicide, 68, (*fig.*) 67, (*table*) 68
Childbearing, and mental disorder, 75–78, 134
Childhood mourning, 116–18
Children, depression and, 78, 116–18, 125–26
Cholecystectomy, and mental illness, 75
Chronic anterior pituitary failure, 114
Classification, depressive disorders, 13–14, (*tables*) 137, 138
Community stability, and mental disorders, 81, 88
Community surveys: and depressive symptoms, 47–48; and incidence, 48–50; and period prevalence, 43–45, (*table*) 44; and point prevalence, 41–43, (*table*) 42
Compulsion, 5
Constitutional factors, 97
Convulsive therapy, 93
Cornell Medical Index (CMI), 26
Cortisol, 106, 113
Cross-cultural studies, and depression, 81–82
Cushing's syndrome, 107, 113

Definitions: of depressive disorders, 9–10; of mental disorders, 7–8
Dementia praecox, 4, 79, 101; and suicide, 68, (*fig.*) 67, (*table*) 68; and urbanization, 90. *See also* Schizophrenia
Depression: and Addison's disease, 107, 114; and adrenal hormones, 106–7; in Africa, 82; and age, 78–80; and aggression, 126; anaclitic, 78; and animal hibernation, 125; catecholamine metabolism and, 105–6; characteristics of, 14–15; in children, 78–79, 126; clinical typing of, 14–15; defined, 1–2, 6–9, 131–32; diagnosis of, 14–26; drug-induced, 114; electrolyte metabolism and, 108; and female endocrine-physiologic processes, 74; and guilt, 126–29; history of, 2–6; in India, 82–83; in infants, 116; and Japanese, 81; in men, 73–78; and menstrual psychosis, 74; and old people, 79; and physical conditions, 112–14; prospective studies of, 134; psychoanalytic concepts of, 119–29; psychodynamic interpretations, 135; and puberty, 78–79; recurrences of, 133; reliability of diagnosis, 17–24; retrospective studies of, 134–36; and separation, 114; and sex, 73–78; and suicide, 74, 78–79, 133, (*tables*) 143, 144; survivorship of, 133–34; in women, 73–78
Depressive disorders: classified, 13–14, (*tables*) 137, 138; cross-cultural studies of, 81; diagnosed cases, 45–46; and early development, 114–19; first admissions to hospitals, (*table*) 51; among Negroes, 84–86; patients, 46–47; period prevalence of, 43–45, (*table*) 44; point prevalence of, 41–43, (*table*) 42; and time trends, 29–37, (*fig.*) 31, (*tables*) 32, 34; race, 84–86; and social class, 88; and suicide, 55–71, (*figs.*) 63, 67, (*tables*) 65, 68; treatment for, 93–96; types of, 9–10
Depressive neurosis, definition, 10
Depressive psychoneurosis, definition, 10
Depressive reaction, definition, 10
Depressive symptoms, 47–48
Diagnosis: of depression, 14–26;

INDEX

differential, 16–17; reliability of, 17–24; techniques of, 24–26
Diagnostic and Statistical Manual, Mental Disorders (1952), 7, 12
Divorced persons, and suicide, 58
Dominant-gene hypothesis, 100
Drug-induced depression, 114
Drugs, antidepressant, 93–94, 105
Dysthymia, 4

Early infancy, 78, 125
Ego, conflict within, 124
Einheitspsychose, 3
Electroconvulsive therapy, 93, 96
Electrolyte disturbances, 113
Electrolyte metabolism, 108
Endocrine disorders, 113
Endocrine physiology, and depression, 74
Endogenous depression, definition, 9
Endogenous psychosis, definition, 9
Epinephrine, 106
Ethnicity, and mental illness, 80–86
Euphoria, 15, 114
Exogenous depression, 9
Exogenous psychosis, definition, 9
Extra-pyramidal disturbance, 113

False melancholia, 2–3
Family stability, and mental disorders, 88
Fertility, and manic depression, 89–90
Folie circulaire, la, 3, 5
Functional psychotic disorders, 8
Future research, 131–36

Genetics, behavior, 97–98; psychiatric, 38–39, 98–101
Group for the Advancement of Psychiatry, 18, 27
Guilt, 128
Guilt feelings, 14, 126–29

Handbook of Psychiatric Rating Scales, 25
Hereditary alienation, 5

Heredity: and manic-depressive psychosis, 98–104; and mental disorder, 97–105
Hibernation of animals, 125
Hospital depression and suicide rates, 66
17-Hydroxycorticosteroids (17-OH-CS), 106–7
Hypopituitarism, 114
Hysterectomy, and mental disorder, 74–75

Iceland disease (myalgic encephalomyelitis), 113
Imipramine-like agents, 105
Immigrants, and mental illness, 83, 84
Incidence of mental disorder, 37–38, 48–53
India, depression in, 82–83
Infant depression, 116
Infectious hepatitis, 113
Infectious mononucleosis, 113
Influenza psychoses, 112–13
International Classification of Diseases (*International List of Causes of Death*), 11, 21
Involutional melancholia, 13, 104; defined, 9; median age for, 79, 80; and suicide, 67, 68, (*fig.*) 67, (*table*) 68
Involutional psychosis, 9, 85, 103; first hospitalization, (*table*) 34

Japanese, depression and suicide among, 81

Leukemia, 114
Lifetime prevalence, 37
Lithium, 59, 108

Mania, 2, 35, 123
Manic behavior, and lithium, 95
Manic-depressive link, 108–11
Manic-depressive psychosis, 35–6, 85, 104, 108; and age, 87; defined, 9; and depression-elation response, 109–10; dominant-gene hypothesis and, 100; and en-

vironment, 119; and fertility, 89–90; first hospitalization for, (*table*) 34; and marital status, 89–90, (*table*) 146; median age for, 79; and men, 87; morbidity risk for, 99–101; and Negroes, 87; postpartum, 76–77; and pregnancy, 77; and psychoanalysis, 120; and schizophrenia, 16–17; by sex, (*table*) 146; and social class, 86–87; and suicide, 63, 67, 68, 69, (*fig.*) 67, (*table*) 68; symptoms of, 15; and twinning, 102–3, (*table*) 147; and urbanization, 90; and women, 87

Marital status: and mental illness, 89–90; and schizophrenia, (*table*) 146; and manic-depressive psychosis, (*table*) 146; and suicide, 57–58

Melancholia, 1, 4, 121–22, 123; history of, 2–3; terminology of, 5

Men: and depression, 73–78, 87; and suicide, 74

"Menstrual psychosis," and depression, 74

Mental disorder. *See* Depression; Depressive disorders; Manic-depressive psychosis; Schizophrenia

Mental hospitals, 29, 30–34, (*fig.*) 31, (*table*) 32

Midtown Manhattan Study (1953–54), 47

Migration, and mental illness, 83–84

Monoamine oxidase inhibitors, 105

Morbidity trends, 27–53

Mortality, and depression, 55–71

Mourning, 120–21

"Mourning and Melancholia" (S. Freud), 120

Myalgic encephalomyelitis (Iceland disease), 113

Myocardial infarction, 114

National Committee of Mental Hygiene, 12

National Institute of Mental Health, 28–29, 52

Negroes: and depression, 84–87; and suicide, 57

Norepinephrine, 105, 106

Obsessional neurosis, 123

Occupation, and mental illness, 90–91

Osteoarthritis, 114

Paranoia, first hospitalization for, (*table*) 34

Parentage, and mental disease, 83–84

Parental deprivation (children's), 117–18

Paresis, general: and immigrants, 83; and suicide, 67

Pellagra, 113

Period prevalence, 37; and community surveys, 43–45, (*table*) 44

Periodic insanity, 4

Pernicious anemia, 114

Personality disorders, 7–8

"Personality illnesses," 5

Pharmacotherapy, 93–94

Phenothiazines, 114

Physical conditions, and mental disorder, 112–14

Point prevalence, 37; and community surveys, 41–43, (*table*) 42

Population groups, general, depressive symptoms in, 47–48

Postpartum manic depression, 76–77

Postpartum mental disorder, 75–78

Potassium deficiency, 113

Pregnancy: and depression, 77; and schizophrenia, 77

Prevalence of mental disorder, 37–53

Psychiatric case registers, 45–46

Psychiatric genetics, 98–101

Psychiatric interview, 24–25

INDEX

Psychoanalysis, 120
Psychobiologic Unit of the Standard Nomenclature of Diseases, 13
Psychodynamics, 119–29
Psychogenic psychosis, definition, 10
Psychologic tests, 25
Psychoneuroses, 6, 85; defined, 7; and psychosis, 8
Psychoses, 5, 13, 83; defined, 7, 9; and psychoneurosis, 8; and social class, 88
Psychosurgery, 93
Psychotherapy, 93
Psychotic depressive reaction, definition, 9
Puberty, and depression, 78–79

"Raging melancholy," 3
Reaction types (Meyer), 5
Reactive depressive psychosis, 9, 10, 13
Recessive gene hypothesis, 101
Reliability of diagnosis, 17–24
Religion, and suicide, 58
Research, perspectives for, 131–36
Reserpine, 114
Retarded adults, 113

Schizo-affective psychosis, definition, 10
Schizophrenia, 132; and stability, 88; first hospitalization, (*table*) 34, 146; hereditary morbidity risk for, 103; and immigrants, 83, 84; and manic depression, 16–17; median age for, 79; and pregnancy, 77; and social class, 87, 88; and suicide, 67; and young people, 79
Seasonality: of mental illness, 92–93; of suicide, 58
Separation, and depression, 114
Serotonin, 105
Sex: differences in, and depression, 73–78, (*table*) 146; and schizophrenia, (*table*) 146
Single persons, and suicide, 58

Social class: and depressive disorders, 86–88; and schizophrenia, 87, 88; and suicide, 59
Stirling County (Canada) Study, 47
Suicide: and alcoholism, 67, (*table*) 68; attempted, 14, 69–71; and cerebral arteriosclerosis, 68, (*fig.*) 67, (*table*) 68; and children, 78–79, 117–18; and dementia praecox, 68, (*fig.*) 67, (*table*) 68; and depression, 78–79, 133; and depressive mental illness, 55–71, (*figs.*) 63, 67, (*tables*) 64, 68; and divorced persons, 58; and general paresis, 67; and hospital population, 66; and involutional melancholia, 67, 68, (*fig.*) 67, (*table*) 68; among Japanese, 81; and manic-depressives, 63, 67, 68, 69, (*table*) 68; manipulative, 60; and marital status, 57–58; and melancholia, 62; in men, 74; and mental illness, 61–62; among Negroes, 57; and psychotic depressive illness, 66; and puberty, 78–79; rates, 56–59, (*figs.*) 149, 150, (*tables*) 143, 144; and religion, 58; and schizophrenia, 67; seasonality of, 58; and single persons, 58; and socioeconomic status, 59; trends and factors in, 56–60; and unemployment, 59; urban-rural comparisons, 58; and white population, 57; and widows, 58; and women, 74

Tests, psychologic, 25–26
Treatment, 93–96
Tuberculosis in twins, (*table*) 148
Twins: and depression, 102–3, (*table*) 147; and tuberculosis, (*table*) 148

Unemployment, and suicide, 59
United States, suicide rates in, 56–57, 58
Urban-rural comparisons: and

mental illness, 90–91; and suicide, 58

Widows: and mental illness, 89; and suicide, 58

Women: depression in, 73–78; suicide among, 74

World Health Organization Expert Committee on Mental Health, 11–12

Designed by Arlene J. Sheer

Composed in Linotype Times Roman and Times Roman Bold by The Colonial Press Inc.

Printed letterpress by The Colonial Press Inc. on 60-lb. Perkins & Squier R

Bound by The Colonial Press Inc. in Columbia Riverside Chambray